PATHWAYS

SECOND EDITION

Listening, Speaking, and Critical Thinking

Teacher's Guide

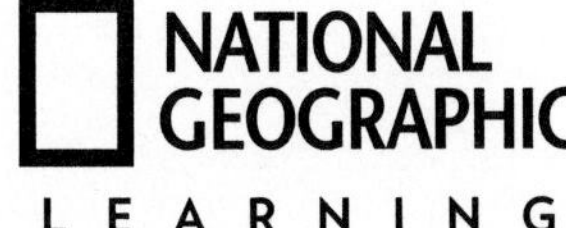

Australia • Brazil • Mexico • Singapore • United Kingdom • United States

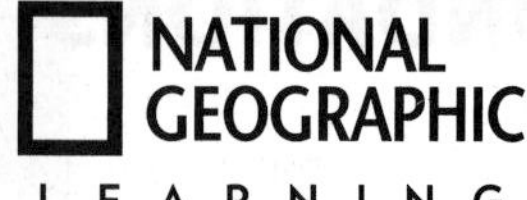

Pathways Teacher's Guide Foundations, Listening, Speaking, and Critical Thinking, Second Edition

Cynthia Fettig and Kathy Najafi

Publisher: Sherrise Roehr

Executive Editor: Laura Le Dréan

Managing Editor: Jennifer Monaghan

Senior Development Editor: Eve Einselen Yu

Associate Development Editors: Lisl Bove and Jennifer Williams-Rapa

Director of Global and U.S. Marketing: Ian Martin

Product Marketing Manager: Tracy Bailie

Media Research: Leila Hishmeh

Senior Director, Production: Michael Burggren

Manager, Production: Daisy Sosa

Content Project Manager: Mark Rzeszutek

Senior Digital Product Manager: Scott Rule

Manufacturing Planner: Mary Beth Hennebury

Interior and Cover Design: Brenda Carmichael

Art Director: Brenda Carmichael

Composition: MPS North America LLC

ISBN-13: 978-1-337-56245-4

National Geographic Learning
20 Channel Center Street
Boston, MA 02210
USA

National Geographic Learning, a Cengage Learning Company, has a mission to bring the world to the classroom and the classroom to life. With our English language programs, students learn about their world by experiencing it. Through our partnerships with National Geographic and TED Talks, they develop the language and skills they need to be successful global citizens and leaders.

Locate your local office at **international.cengage.com/region**

Visit National Geographic Learning online at **NGL.Cengage.com/ELT**
Visit our corporate website at **www.cengage.com**

Printed in the United States of America

Print Number: 02 Print Year: 2018

TABLE OF CONTENTS

TEACHING WITH *PATHWAYS*

In *Pathways Listening, Speaking, and Critical Thinking, Second Edition*, real-world content from National Geographic provides a context for meaningful language acquisition. Each unit's authentic, relevant, and high-interest content is designed to motivate both students and teachers alike. Students will learn essential vocabulary, review important grammatical structures, and practice listening and speaking skills that will allow them to succeed in academic settings.

Each unit of *Pathways Listening, Speaking, and Critical Thinking* features:

- Academic Skills objectives listed at the start of each unit.
- Explore the Theme pages that introduce the unit theme while developing visual literacy skills.
- Target vocabulary presented in interesting and varied contexts.
- Extensive audio program including lectures, interviews, conversations, podcasts, and pronunciation models that expose students to different genres and speakers.
- Skills boxes that instruct students on key vocabulary, listening, note-taking, speaking, pronunciation, grammar, and presentation skills.
- A Critical Thinking focus in every unit, in addition to activities that practice a variety of critical thinking skills.
- Lesson and Final Tasks that get students to synthesize language, skills, and content, and to apply this knowledge to topics of interest to them.
- A Reflection section that encourages students to reflect on what they have learned.

The *Pathways* series is flexible and designed to be used in a wide variety of language-learning programs, from high schools and community colleges, to private language institutes and intensive English programs. A Pacing Guide for implementing the program in various teaching situations is provided on page xii. In addition to the student book, the *Pathways* series offers an Online Workbook where students can get extra listening practice with additional audio, watch the National Geographic videos, and work on 20 additional activities per unit that reinforce the skills introduced in the book.

Teaching Academic Literacy

In addition to teaching essential listening and speaking skills, the *Pathways* series promotes other aspects of academic literacy that will help students succeed in an academic setting, such as:

- visual literacy
- critical thinking
- collaboration skills
- presentation skills
- digital literacy

Students build essential academic literacy skills while encountering fascinating stories about real people and places around the world. The use of informative, relevant, and authoritative content from National Geographic builds global and cultural awareness, and develops learners' understanding of important 21st century issues that affect us all. While these skills are components of academic literacy, they will also serve students in their work lives as well.

Increasing Visual Literacy

Photographs, maps, charts, and graphs can all convey enormous amounts of information, and it is essential for students to be able to make sense of them. *Pathways* uses high quality visuals to help students develop the ability to interpret and discuss visual information.

STIMULATING INFOGRAPHICS from National Geographic publications help explain complex processes.

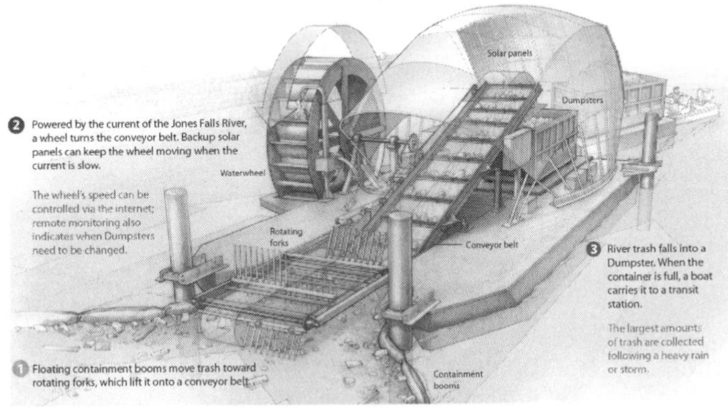

CHARTS AND GRAPHS present numerical information visually.

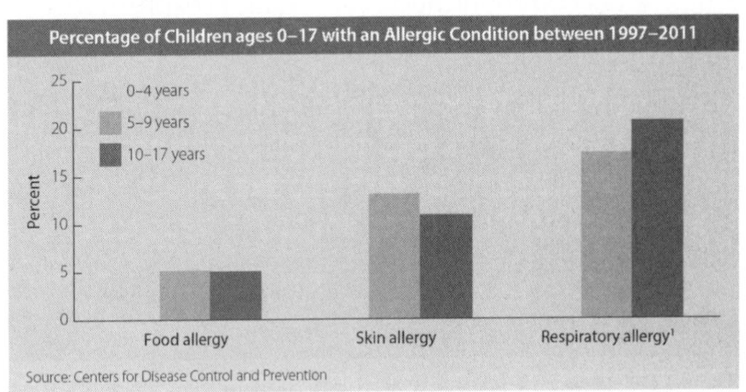

MAPS show locations and geographical features, and illustrate historical facts and current trends.

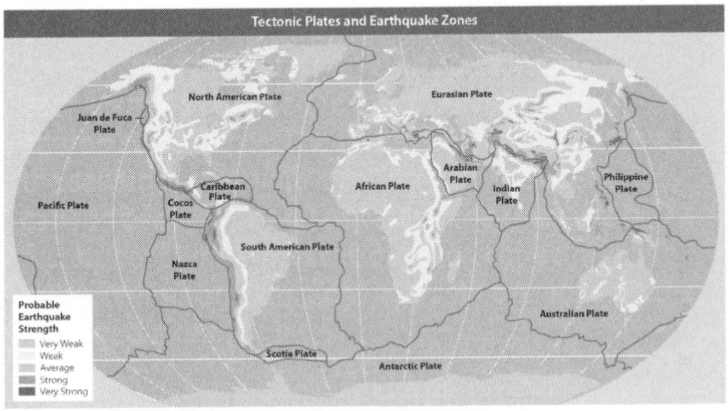

Tectonic Plates and Earthquake Zones

North American Plate
Eurasian Plate
Juan de Fuca Plate
Arabian Plate
Philippine Plate
Caribbean Plate
African Plate
Indian Plate
Pacific Plate
Cocos Plate
South American Plate
Nazca Plate
Australian Plate
Scotia Plate
Antarctic Plate
Probable Earthquake Strength
Very Weak
Weak
Average
Strong
Very Strong

"The Geography of Transport Systems" https://people.hofstra. edu/geotrans /eng/ch9en/conc9en/plate_tectonics.html

GRAPHIC ORGANIZERS show the relationships between ideas.

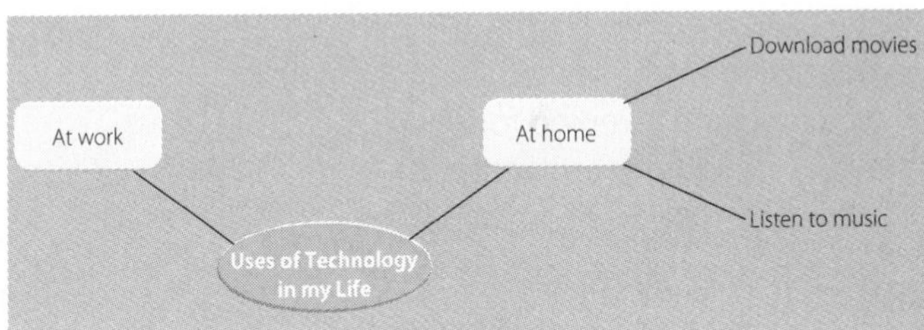

Using Videos

Pathways uses videos from National Geographic's award-winning film collection. They present a unique and visually dynamic perspective on the unit theme.

Teaching Video-Viewing Skills

Videos differ from listening passages in important ways. Because students are processing more than just words, extra layers of meaning need to be understood such as:

- information about the video's setting;
- signs and captions identifying people or places;
- maps and diagrams explaining information and processes;
- nonverbal communication such as facial expressions, gestures, and body language;
- music and sound effects.

All *Pathways* videos come with the option to use English subtitles, and with full English transcripts that can be found at the end of this teacher's guide.

The Video Section

Each unit features activities for students to do *before, while*, and *after* watching the video.

BEFORE VIEWING

This section provides background knowledge and stimulates interest in the topic. Activities include:

- pre-teaching vocabulary from the video;
- providing background information about the topic;
- predicting video content using images and captions.

WHILE VIEWING

As they watch the video, students complete activities such as:

- checking their predictions;
- identifying main ideas;
- watching and listening for details;
- inferring opinions and attitudes.

AFTER VIEWING

Students check comprehension and relate the video to other aspects of the unit and their own lives by completing activities such as:

- analyzing the sequence of events in the video;
- applying the ideas in the videos to their communities;
- synthesizing information from the video and information from the listening passage.

Building Critical Thinking Skills

Students today are expected to do more than just learn and memorize information. The ability to think critically about a topic—to analyze, apply, and evaluate ideas—is increasingly essential in an academic setting. *Pathways* actively fosters critical thinking while students complete listening and speaking activities.

Critical Thinking and Language

Critical thinking requires a deep processing of language, which aids in language acquisition. Articulating complex responses requires creative thought and word associations, which lead to better comprehension and retention of target language.

These are some of the critical thinking skills covered in *Pathways*:

- **Analyzing** a passage in close detail in order to identify key points, similarities, and differences.
- **Applying** information to a different context e.g., applying possible solutions to problems.
- **Evaluating** how relevant, important, or useful something is. This involves, for example, looking carefully at the sources of information, or the reasons the speaker provides for or against something.
- **Inferring** what a speaker is saying indirectly, or implicitly, rather than directly, or explicitly.
- **Synthesizing** appropriate information and ideas from more than one source to make a judgment, summary, or conclusion based on the evidence.
- **Reflecting** on ideas and information in a text in order to relate them to your own personal experience and viewpoints, and to form your own opinion.

While each unit contains several opportunities for critical thinking, there is also a Critical Thinking Focus in every unit:

> **CRITICAL THINKING** Synthesizing
>
> When you synthesize, you combine, or put together, information from two or more sources in order to understand a topic in a new way. This can also involve combining new information with your own ideas and knowledge about a topic. Synthesizing can help you find a solution to a problem or think of new ways of doing or improving something.

Preparing for Standardized Tests

Pathways is designed to provide practice for standardized exams, such as IELTS and TOEFL. Many activities practice or focus on key exam skills needed for test success. In the student book you will find an index of activities that are similar to common question types found in these tests.

Frequently Asked Questions

How are the Student Book units organized?

Foundations includes eight units, while levels 1-4 each include 10 units.

Each unit consists of seven main sections:

Vocabulary A, Listening A, Speaking A, Video, Vocabulary B, Listening B, and Speaking B

The unit opens with an introduction to the unit theme. The vocabulary, listening passages, and videos that follow, together with their corresponding exercises, then build towards a final speaking task that synthesizes the skills, topics, and language presented and practiced in the unit.

Will my students be able to handle the themes in the book?

The content and language are graded so that students can come into the series with little or no background information.

Each unit starts with a Think and Discuss page. This consists of a compelling photograph and questions designed to spark students' curiosity about the theme. The Explore the Theme spread further engages students and taps into their critical thinking with a thought-provoking angle on the theme presented through photos, text, and infographics.

As students progress through a unit, exercises and activities further add to students' knowledge of the theme. So, by the time students get to the final speaking task, they have enough language and information to speak with confidence about the topic.

How are Listenings A and B related?

The two listenings offer different perspectives on the unit theme. They consist of contrasting listening types, for example, one might be lecture by a university professor, and the other a conversation among students. The variety of listening passages is designed to mirror the range that learners will encounter in academic and real-world settings.

How does the series build vocabulary skills?

Each listening passage contains ten high-frequency vocabulary items (eight in *Foundations)*. These are introduced in the Vocabulary sections, which focus on developing students' ability to use contextual clues to determine meaning. Target words are then reinforced and recycled throughout the series.

How are listening and speaking integrated in the series?

All of the sections and exercises in each unit are thematically linked. Listenings A and B and their corresponding activities present and reinforce ideas, vocabulary, and grammar that students will use in their Speaking activities. For example, students may learn to listen for problems and solutions in the Listening section, and then role-play a conversation in which they analyze problems and offer solutions in the final speaking task. Or students may hear about explorers in a listening passage, and then be asked to talk about a place they would like to explore.

How does *Pathways* develop listening and speaking skills?

Each unit of *Pathways Listening, Speaking, and Critical Thinking* contains two listening sections. The language in the listening passages represents realistic situations, yet the language is controlled for level, and students may listen to each passage more than once. This guided listening gives students the chance to practice listening and note-taking skills and to develop the confidence and fluency they'll need before they are immersed in an academic setting.

Each Listening section contains three parts:

- Before Listening activities provide background information and explicit instruction in listening skills.
- While Listening activities give students practice in listening for main ideas and details, and in making inferences.
- After Listening activities are designed to reinforce listening skills by allowing students to discuss and react to the listening passage.

Every section of *Pathways Listening, Speaking, and Critical Thinking* provides opportunities for classroom speaking and discussion, often in pairs or in small groups. Frequent classroom discussions and interactions prepare students to participate in class and succeed in an academic setting. In the Speaking sections, striking images and brief stories about real people and places often provide the content for engaging interactions. Speaking activities are designed with a scaffolded approach. They progress from controlled and guided activities to more open and communicative activities. Early confidence-building motivates students to attempt activities that increase in difficulty, taking them to their ultimate goal—participation in authentic speaking activities such as classroom presentations, formal discussions, and debates.

The Speaking sections contain:

- Clear and succinct grammar boxes which give students a single language structure to concentrate on. The grammar points lend themselves to discussion of the unit theme and can be recycled throughout the unit.
- A Presentation Skill box at points where students give presentations, so they provide immediate practice of skills needed for planning and delivering successful oral presentations.
- An Everyday Language box that provides tips and expressions to help students develop the language they will need for class work and in their day-to-day exchanges.
- A Speaking Task. The Lesson Task and Final Task are consolidating speaking activities. They often involve collaboration with a partner or a group as well as an oral presentation of results or ideas.

The *MyELT* online workbook provides additional guided listening and speaking tasks that build on the skills and language learners have developed in the Student Book unit.

How does the *Listening, Speaking, and Critical Thinking* strand align with the *Reading, Writing, and Critical Thinking* strand?

The content in each unit is related to the content in the corresponding strand. For example, Level 1, Unit 3 "The Marketing Machine" in the *Listening and Speaking* strand is about business and marketing, while Level 1, Unit 3 "Why We Buy" in the *Reading and Writing* strand is about the psychology of business and marketing. Language has also been controlled and recycled so that students meet similar structures and vocabulary across the two strands.

SPEAKING ASSESSMENT RUBRIC

Rating	General Description	Pronunciation & Fluency	Vocabulary	Topic Development
4	The student speaks smoothly and effectively, similar to a native speaker.	The student's pronunciation is similar to a native speaker's. S/he speaks clearly and articulately with little or no hesitation.	The student's vocabulary is sophisticated and similar to a native speaker's.	The student's content reflects a deep understanding of the topic.
3	The student can express him/herself with relative ease and fluency and very few errors.	The student's pronunciation is clear, with few errors. S/he is able to respond to the prompt with relative ease.	The student's vocabulary enhances his or her response to the prompt.	The student's content is relevant to the topic and shows a good understanding.
2	The student is generally able to make him/herself understood, with some hesitation and errors.	The student is inconsistent in his or her pronunciation. The student demonstrates some fluency and is able to put together simple sentences.	The student's vocabulary relates to the topic, but is basic and with a few errors.	The student's content has some relevance to the topic, but is not well developed.
1	The student's response is very limited in content &/or coherence.	The student struggles to pronounce words and has difficulty putting words together to form a sentence.	The student's vocabulary is limited to high frequency words.	The student's content is minimally relevant to the topic or prompt.
0 The student does not respond, or the response is unrelated to the prompt.				

USING THE TEACHER'S GUIDE

Each unit of this Teacher's Guide contains:

- A list of the academic skills covered in the unit.
- An overview of the unit theme, the listening passages, the video, and the Final Task.
- Suggestions for online search terms for additional information about topics in the unit.
- Teaching notes for each exercise.
- Answer keys.

Other features include:

Recommended Time Frames

Look for the small clock icon with recommended times for completing various tasks. While the recommended total time required for each unit is about six class hours, this will of course vary depending on your particular teaching situation. Likewise, the time allocated for specific sections should be used more as a guide than as a rule. Refer to the Pacing Guide on the following page for a more detailed breakdown.

Ideas for...EXPANSION

These boxes contain suggestions for extra classroom activities that can be used when students need additional support, have a high level of interest in the topic, or when there is an opportunity to explore a different aspect of the unit theme.

Ideas for...PRESENTING THE SKILL

These boxes provide a variety of ways to introduce the skill being taught as well as practical suggestions for quick activities to put the skill in use.

Ideas for...CHECKING COMPREHENSION

These boxes offer additional suggestions for assessing students' comprehension during class and provide exercises to check for understanding.

Ideas for...MULTI-LEVEL CLASSES

These boxes provide techniques for use in mixed-ability classrooms, where learner diversity can benefit everyone in the class.

TIPS

These supplementary teaching tips are general suggestions to facilitate classroom management, such as asking student volunteers to record answers on the board as you lead a discussion.

In addition, this teacher's guide also contains ***Audio Scripts*** and ***Video Scripts***, which can be found at the back of this book.

Use these for a more detailed study of the audio and video content. The scripts, for example, can be provided to students for additional comprehension practice before or after they listen to the passage or view the video.

PACING GUIDE

One unit of *Pathways Listening, Speaking, and Critical Thinking* typically requires six hours to complete. A *Pathways* unit can be adapted to shorter class durations by setting aside some activities as homework, or to longer class durations by using follow-up questions and expansion activities from the Teacher's Guide, and/or activities from the Online Workbook:

Total course length: 45 hours	Total course length: 45 hours	Total course length: 60 hours	Total course length: 60 hours
– 60-minute class: 1 unit in 6 classes	– 90-minute class: 1 unit in 4 classes	– 60-minute class: 1 unit in 6 classes	– 90-minute class: 1 unit in 4 classes
To cover the entire student book and make time for some expansion activities: – The Vocabulary activities can be assigned as homework and reviewed in class. – The Video can be assigned as homework and reviewed in class. – Listening A or B can be assigned as homework and reviewed in class.	To cover the entire student book and make time for some expansion activities: – The Vocabulary activities can be assigned as homework and reviewed in class. – The Video can be assigned as homework and reviewed in class. – Listening A or B can be assigned as homework and reviewed in class.	There is enough time to complete the entire student book in class. In addition: – Some follow-up questions and expansion activities in the Teacher's Guide can be used. – Online Workbook activities can be done in a lab setting. – ExamView unit tests can be done in class.	There is enough time to complete the entire student book in class. In addition: – Some follow-up questions and expansion activities in the Teacher's Guide can be used. – Online Workbook activities can be done in a lab setting. – ExamView unit tests can be done in class.
Class 1: Think and Discuss Explore the Theme A: Vocabulary **Class 2:** A: Listening A: Speaking (begin) **Class 3:** A: Speaking (finish) Lesson Task **Class 4:** Video B: Vocabulary (begin) **Class 5:** B: Vocabulary (finish) B: Listening **Class 6:** B: Speaking Final Task	**Class 1:** Think and Discuss Explore the Theme A: Vocabulary A: Listening **Class 2:** A: Speaking Lesson Task **Class 3:** Video B: Vocabulary B: Listening (begin) **Class 4:** B: Listening (finish) B: Speaking Final Task	**Class 1:** Think and Discuss Explore the Theme A: Vocabulary **Class 2:** A: Listening A: Speaking (begin) **Class 3:** A: Speaking (finish) Lesson Task **Class 4:** Video B: Vocabulary (begin) **Class 5:** B: Vocabulary (finish) B: Listening **Class 6:** B: Speaking Final Task	**Class 1:** Think and Discuss Explore the Theme A: Vocabulary A: Listening **Class 2:** A: Speaking Lesson Task **Class 3:** Video B: Vocabulary B: Listening (begin) **Class 4:** B: Listening (finish) B: Speaking Final Task

SAME AND DIFFERENT 1

ACADEMIC TRACK

Sociology

ACADEMIC SKILLS

LISTENING	Listening for Main Ideas
	Using a Venn Diagram
SPEAKING	Making Small Talk
	Contractions with *Be*
CRITICAL THINKING	Activating Prior Knowledge

UNIT OVERVIEW

The theme of this unit is how people and/or cultures are both the same and different from one another. The unit provides opportunities for students to share aspects of their lives as well as find out what is the same and different about one another's lives and countries around the world.

- **LISTENING A** **A Lecture on Twins:** A classroom lecture about the similarities and differences in twins. The Jim Twins are used as an example.
- **VIDEO** ***Coming of Age*:** Many countries have a coming-of-age celebration or customs that mark the entrance of a child into adulthood. This coming-of-age story tells about a Fulani boy on his eight-month journey to become a man. The boys of this nomadic people must show they are men by caring for and transferring a herd of cows to a new destination during the rainy season.
- **LISTENING B** **A Conversation about the Teenage Brain:** A professor and a student have a conversation about how the teenage brain develops and the things that can influence a teenager.

For the final task, students draw upon what they have learned in the unit to give a presentation about the aspects of their lives that influence who they are. After creating a pie chart and giving a percentage for how important various aspects of their lives are, students prepare a presentation and deliver it to the class.

For additional information about the topics in this unit, here are some suggestions for online search terms: *coming of age traditions, most popular sports in the world, identical twins, the "Jim twins," Chris Bashinelli, Fulani people, corpus callosum, frontal cortex, cerebellum, amygdala, the teenage brain*

UNIT OPENER

THINK AND DISCUSS *(page 1)*

Ask guiding questions about the photo, such as: Where are these women from? *(Japan)* How old are they? *(20 years old.)* What are they doing? (*They're celebrating becoming adults.*)

ANSWER KEY

THINK AND DISCUSS *(page 1)*

1. Possible answers: The U.S. considers driving or voting to be markers of adulthood. The age to drive differs by state but is usually 16. You must be 18 to vote.
2. Possible answers: The girls are both wearing traditional clothing for the Coming of Age ceremony in Japan. They have the same style, but different color kimonos (dresses). The flowers in their hair are different colors. The wraps around their necks look the same.
3. Answers will vary.

EXPLORE THE THEME *(pages 2–3)*

In pairs, have students look at the world statistics for the sports shown on the page. Have pairs discuss if these same sports are equally popular in their countries. Have students look up statistics for one other sport. Ask volunteers to share their findings.

ANSWER KEY

EXPLORE THE THEME *(pages 2–3)*

1. Soccer, basketball, cricket. The sport that people love most is soccer.
2. Possible answers:

   Same: They all use balls, they are all team sports, they all use a point system to win.

   Different: You use your feet in soccer; in basketball and cricket, you use your hands. In basketball and soccer, you score points by putting the ball into something (basket/goal); in cricket, you hit the ball and run to score points. In soccer, players kick the ball; in basketball players throw the ball; in cricket players hit the ball with a paddle.
3. Answers will vary.

Lesson A

VOCABULARY

A 1.2 *(page 4)*

Ask a few volunteers to share the meaning of one of the vocabulary words.

B 1.3 **Meaning from Context** *(page 4)*

Play the audio twice if necessary.

> Ideas for... **EXPANSION**
>
> Help students use the new vocabulary by asking questions such as:
> 1. *What's your favorite sport?*
> 2. *What are your hobbies?*
> 3. *What music do you like?*
> 4. *Do you think you are shy or friendly?*
> 5. *Where do you like to go on vacation?*

C *(page 4)*

Pair students up and have them quiz each other on the words and definitions. One student reads the definition and the other student says the word.

> Ideas for... **EXPANSION**
>
> Have students make notecards of the vocabulary words. On one side of the note card, write the vocabulary word, and on the other side, write the definition and a sample sentence.

D *(page 5)*

Recreate the chart on the board and elicit a few more examples of each category from the class.

> Ideas for... **EXPANSION**
>
> Tell students to create a chart in their notebooks with the following categories: school subjects, types of books, and types of food. Tell them to add words for each category and then compare their lists with a partner.

> Ideas for... **PRESENTING THE VOCABULARY SKILL: Collocations**
>
> Explain that a collocation is two or more words that often go together. The words sound natural together. Give the examples: We say, we "speak a language," but we don't say we "say a language."
>
> Explain that word maps can help students recognize and remember collocations. Demonstrate on the board how to create word maps for collocations.
> 1. Write a verb in a circle, e.g., *take*.
> 2. Draw lines out of the circle and write the different nouns that go together with the verb *take* at the end of the lines, e.g., *take a bath, take a test, take turns, take a bus, etc.*
> 3. Repeat this process for the verbs in the *Vocabulary Skill* box.

> Ideas for... **EXPANSION**
>
> To increase students' awareness of collocations, write a few more verbs on the board, e.g., *see, have, make, get*. In pairs, have students choose one verb to work with and create a word map for the collocations related to that verb. Suggest that they look up the verb in a dictionary or on an online site. Ask volunteers to draw their word maps on the board.

E *(page 5)*

TIP Teach students to read a line of a conversation, look up from the page, and say the line to their partner. Doing this requires students to process the language in order to remember the line, and making eye contact while speaking is a natural way to role-play a real conversation.

F **Personalizing** *(page 5)*

Ask volunteer pairs to perform their conversations in front of the class.

ANSWER KEY

VOCABULARY

B *(page 4)* **1.** favorite; **2.** music; **3.** science; **4.** friendly; **5.** kind; **6.** hobby; **7.** shy; **8.** vacation

C *(page 4)* **1.** vacation; **2.** science; **3.** music; **4.** kind; **5.** friendly; **6.** favorite; **7.** shy; **8.** hobby

D *(page 5)* Possible answers are in italic.

Country	Language	Sport	Hobby	Music
Saudi Arabia	English	soccer (UK football)	reading	rock
Brazil	Arabic	volleyball	taking pictures	jazz
United States	Portuguese	*baseball*	*drawing*	pop
China	*Chinese*	*tennis*	*writing poems*	*classical*
Mexico	*Spanish*	*basketball*	*riding bikes*	*rap*

E *(page 5)* **1.** play; **2.** listen to; **3.** watch; **4.** go; **5.** speak; **6.** play; **7.** do; **8.** ride; **9.** go

45 MINS

LISTENING: A LECTURE ON TWINS

BEFORE LISTENING

A Previewing *(page 6)*

Put students in pairs. Give pairs one minute to find as many things that are the same and that are different about the twins in the photo. Then begin the listening section by asking if they know any twins. Ask them to describe their similarities and differences.

B Prior Knowledge *(page 6)*

Ask pairs to share what they discussed with the whole class.

WHILE LISTENING

C 1.4 ▶ 1.1 **Listening for Main Ideas** *(page 6)*

Before playing the audio or slide show, remind students to listen for the two questions from exercise B.

D 1.5 **Listening for Details** *(page 6)*

Ask students to retell any information the professor said in the lecture.

Ideas for... PRESENTING THE NOTE-TAKING SKILL: Using a Venn Diagram

Draw a Venn Diagram on the board. Explain that this diagram is useful to show the things that are the same and the things that are different between two people, things, or ideas. Tell the students to open their books to page 4. With the class, use the photos and the information about the two people on page 4 (Abdul and Claudia) to fill in the sample blank Venn diagram on the board. Elicit what is the same and what is different about them. Write their ideas on the diagram.

E 1.6 **Note Taking** *(page 6)*

Play the audio twice if necessary. Recreate the Venn diagram from the student book on the board. After the pairs have compared their diagrams with each other, elicit the answers and write them in the Venn diagram on the board.

AFTER LISTENING

F Critical Thinking: Reflecting *(page 7)*

Lead a class brainstorming session on the pros and cons of being a twin.

Ideas for... EXPANSION

Tell students to choose two people in the class, two siblings, or two friends and create a Venn diagram about the things that are the same and the things that are different about those two people. This can be done outside of class as homework, or during class time. Divide the class into small groups and have them share their Venn diagrams with their groupmates.

ANSWER KEY

LISTENING

A *(page 6)* Possible answers:

They both have the same hair color, smiles, and general look. The one on the left has a suit on; the one on the right looks more relaxed, less serious.

B *(page 6)* Possible answers:

1. Most identical twins have the same hair color, eye color, and other facial features. They are either both male or both female and their height is often the same. They might have different hair or clothing styles, and they may act differently.
2. Identical twins look the same, but fraternal twins do not; they usually look different. One may be male and the other female. One may have brown hair and the other blonde.

C *(page 6)* Possible answers:

1. Identical twins are from one egg.
2. Fraternal twins are from two eggs.

D *(page 6)*

1. ✓ The two boys lived with different families.

3. ✓ Their wives were named Linda and Betty.

7. ✓ They both named a son James.

E *(page 7)*

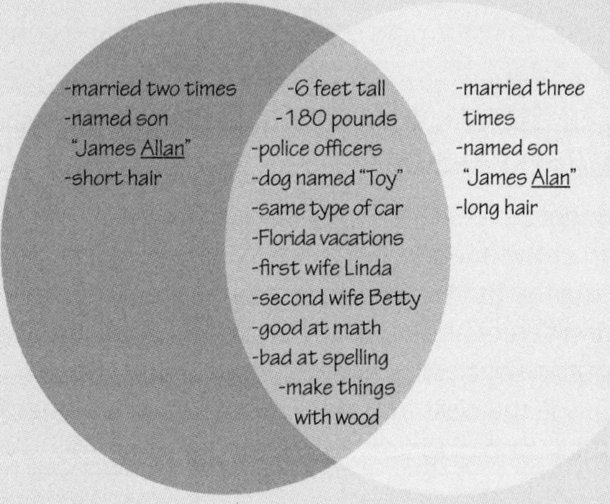

F *(page 7)*

1. Answers will vary.
2. Possible answer: Life might be difficult because people compare them. It might be easy because they have each other as friends.

SPEAKING

Ideas for… PRESENTING GRAMMAR FOR SPEAKING: Simple Present and Past of *Be*

Write the following sentences on the board:

1. I am from Saudi Arabia. // ___________ from Saudi Arabia.
2. He is friendly. // ___________ friendly.
3. You are not Japanese. // ___________ not Japanese.
4. She was not in the room. // She ___________ in the room.
5. They were not cold. // They ___________ cold.

Ask volunteers to read the sentences and come to the board and write in the other way to say the sentence using the contraction. Ask if they know when contractions are typically used (in speaking and informal writing) and when the full form is usually used (in formal writing).

A  1.7 *(page 8)*

Have the students listen and write their answers individually, and then check their answers with a partner.

Ideas for… MULTI-LEVEL CLASSES

For lower level students, have pairs state facts about Chris Bashinelli. For example: *He is a National Geographic Explorer. He was born in New York.*

For higher level students, have pairs ask each other questions (either *Yes/No* questions or *Wh-* Questions) about Chris Bashinelli. For example: *Was Chris born in New York?* Or, *Where was Chris born?*

Ideas for… EXPANSION

Divide the class into pairs. Tell pairs to think of and say three things about a friend or family member using the simple present of *be,* and then to say three things about a friend or family member using the simple past of *be*. Ask for a few volunteers to share their sentences with the class.

B  *(page 9)*

Recreate the chart on the board and write sentences for your own life as an example.

Ideas for... **EXPANSION**

Have students write two truths and a lie about their past or present. Encourage them to write sentences using the simple present or past of *be*. In small groups, students read their three sentences and their groupmates guess which is the lie.

C 1.8 *(page 9)*

Play the audio twice if necessary.

D *(page 9)*

Have two of the students in the group stand up and practice the conversation. The third student observes and gives them ideas for improvement. The groupmates take turns being the observer. After groups have had time to practice, ask for a few volunteer pairs to role-play their conversation in front of the class.

E 1.9 *(page 10)*

Model how to do the activity by doing the first two lines from Conversation 1 with the class. Play the audio twice if necessary.

F *(page 10)*

Have pairs stand up and move around the room, practicing each conversation with a different partner.

ANSWER KEY

SPEAKING

A *(page 8)* **1.** are; **2.** is; **3.** is; **4.** was; **5.** were; **6.** was; **7.** isn't; **8.** wasn't; **9.** are; **10.** aren't; **11.** is; **12.** is

B *(page 9)* Answers will vary.

C *(page 9)* **1.** 'm; **2.** is; **3.** 's; **4.** is; **5.** Are; **6.** 're not/aren't; **7.** 're; **8.** are; **9.** 'm; **10.** Are; **11.** were; **12.** 're; **13.** Are; **14.** was; **15.** 'm; **16.** was

E *(page 10)*

1. Where are you from?
2. What do you do?
3. How about you?
4. Can you believe this weather?
5. Do you play any sports?
6. What are your hobbies?

LESSON TASK: INTERVIEWING A CLASSMATE

A *(page 11)*

- Go over the directions and point out the space in the chart where students write their own information and the space where they take notes on their partner's responses.
- Have students review the interview questions silently and think of their own responses.
- Give students ten minutes to complete the interview (five minutes for each partner). Encourage them to elaborate on their answers while they are talking to each other.

TIP Model the interview activity with a volunteer. Ask the volunteer one or two interview questions and take notes of the answers on the board. Ask follow-up questions to encourage students to give more details.

B *(page 11)*

Be sure students work with the same partners they interviewed in exercise A. Ask a volunteer to explain to the class how to use the Venn diagram. Be sure the explanation includes that the center part is for things that are the same about both people and the sides are for things that are different.

C *(page 11)*

Be sure that two pairs are coming together to form a group of four.

ANSWER KEY

LESSON TASK

A–C *(page 11)* Answers will vary.

Video

VIEWING: *COMING OF AGE*

(page 12)

Overview of the Video

Many countries have a coming-of-age celebration or customs that mark the entrance of a child into adulthood. This coming-of-age story tells about a Fulani boy on his eight-month journey to become a man. The boys of this nomadic people must show they are men by caring for and transferring a herd of cows to a new destination during the rainy season.

BEFORE VIEWING

A *(page 12)*

Read the vocabulary words aloud and have the students repeat after you. Have students match the words to the definitions first, and then check them with the class.

B Prior Knowledge *(page 12)*

Give an example from your country on a coming-of-age custom.

> Ideas for... **MULTI-LEVEL CLASSES**
>
> Lower level students can tell what their custom is for coming of age in their country.
>
> Higher level students can give a short presentation (including photos they find on the Internet) of the coming-of-age custom in their country, or of another one they have researched. This could be done as an at-home assignment or during class time when the teacher is working with lower level students.

C *(page 12)*

Ask students to walk around the room and share their answers with three other students.

TIP Creating opportunities for movement in the class helps break up the monotony of sitting and it helps stimulate the brain. Movement-type activities are considered a part of kinesthetic learning.

D *(page 13)*

Be sure that participants are working with a different partner than they just spoke with in exercise C.

WHILE VIEWING

E ▶ 1.2 **Understanding Main Ideas** *(page 13)*

Stop the video every few minutes to discuss the main ideas and details of the story.

F ▶ 1.2 **Understanding Details** *(page 13)*

Do this exercise by designating two corners in the room as *True* and *False*. Read the statements and have the class walk to either the corner in the room designated as *True*, or the corner designated as *False*.

AFTER VIEWING

G Organizing Ideas *(page 13)*

Before students create their own Venn diagram, provide a model comparing your life to Yoro's life.

H Personalizing *(page 13)*

Put the students in two circles: one circle inside of the other. The students in the inside circle are facing the students in the outside circle. Read the questions aloud from exercise H (along with the ones listed below). Instruct the students in the two circles to align with someone in the other circle to discuss the question. After a minute turn on and off the lights to indicate that students are to move to the next person in the circle for the next question. Then read the next question for students to discuss.

ANSWER KEY

VIDEO

A *(page 12)* **1.** d; **2.** a; **3.** e; **4.** b; **5.** c

B *(page 12)* Answers will vary.

D *(page 13)* Answers will vary.

E *(page 13)* Possible answer: Fulani boys have to take their cows on a trip during the wet season. The cows cannot stay there when there's a lot of water, so the boys travel with the cows to the Sahel Desert, near the Sahara, to find food for them. They return home after about eight months. If their cows look good, then the boys have "come of age" or become men.

F *(page 13)* **1.** T; **2.** F; **3.** F; **4.** T; **5.** T

G *(page 13)* Answers will vary.

H *(page 13)* Note: In the United States, both girls and boys can vote at age 18, and can usually drive at age 16. Also, in some places, especially the South, some families celebrate their daughter's 16th birthday with a "Sweet 16" party.

Lesson B

VOCABULARY

A 1.10 **Meaning from Context** *(page 14)*

After listening to the words, read them aloud and ask the class to repeat after you. Ask volunteers to give a definition or a sample sentence with the words.

> Ideas for... **CHECKING COMPREHENSION**
>
> Check students' understanding of the vocabulary words by having them discuss the following questions in small groups:
>
> 1. What is good about being an *adult*?
> 2. What is good about being a *teenager*?
> 3. What *changes* when you become an adult?
> 4. How does a *typical* teenager act in your country?
> 5. Describe your *parents*.

B 1.11 **Meaning from Context** *(page 14)*

After playing the audio, discuss each quiz question with the class.

> Ideas for... **EXPANSION**
>
> Give students time to write one multiple choice quiz question for the class about a typical person in their country. Encourage them to use a vocabulary word from this unit in their quiz question. Tell them to write their quiz question on the board and have the class answer all the questions. Have the student who wrote it share the answer with the class.

C *(page 15)*

Ask for volunteers to give the answers aloud. Discuss any questions students have about the vocabulary.

> Ideas for... **EXPANSION**
>
> Play a game with the vocabulary words from this unit (Lesson A, Lesson B, and the vocabulary from the Video). Write all the words on the board. Divide the class into two or three teams. Give a definition for one of the words listed on the board. The first person from each team runs to the board and "swats" the word being defined. Whoever swats the word first, wins a point for his/her team. Continue with other definitions until everyone has had at least two turns.

D **Personalizing** *(page 15)*

Ask students to think of one other quiz question to ask the class.

E **Critical Thinking: Reflecting** *(page 15)*

Be sure students pair up with different partners. Working with various partners can provide more opportunities for improving listening and pronunciation skills.

TIP Always provide a model for how to do an activity before the students do it on their own. Using your own personal information as a model helps students know how to do the activity.

ANSWER KEY

VOCABULARY

B *(page 14)* **1.** 5 feet 11 inches; 5 feet 4 inches; **2.** 86, 45; **3.** 15, 21; **4.** 69, 87; **5.** 30, 100; **6.** 80, 30

C *(page 15)* **1.** adult; **2.** change; **3.** teenager; **4.** grow up; **5.** typical; **6.** parents; **7.** the world; **8.** years old

D–E *(page 15)* Answers will vary.

LISTENING: A CONVERSATION ABOUT THE TEENAGE BRAIN

A **Prior Knowledge** *(page 16)*

Start by eliciting a few ideas together as a class. Have some ideas ready to share in case students don't have any to begin. Then give students more time to make their own lists. Ask for volunteers to share their ideas.

B **Critical Thinking: Analyzing a Visual** *(page 16)*

Review the answers with the class.

> Ideas for... **EXPANSION**
>
> Have students come up with other *True/False* questions about the illustration of the teenage brain. Tell them to read aloud or write their questions on the board for all to answer. Have the student who created the question give the answer.

WHILE LISTENING

C 1.12 **Listening for Main Ideas** *(page 17)*

Play the audio a second time to allow students to check their answers. Review answers as a class.

Ideas for... **PRESENTING THE LISTENING SKILL: LISTENING FOR MAIN IDEAS**

Complete this short activity to check students' understanding of main ideas and details. Write the following sentences on the board. In pairs, have students discuss which part of the example sentences is the main idea and which part provides the details.

1. *The world now has over seven billion people. China and India have the largest populations in the world.*
2. *Typical means different things in different countries. A typical Japanese woman lives to be 86 years old, but in Afghanistan, a typical woman lives to be 45 years old.*

Answers:

1. Main idea: *The world has over seven billion people.* Details: *China and India have the largest populations in the world.*
2. Main idea: *Typical means different things in different countries.* Details: *A typical Japanese woman lives to be 86 years old, but in Afghanistan, a typical woman lives to be 45 years old.*

Tell them that the main idea typically comes first and important words are often repeated several times. Details follow.

D 1.12 **Listening for Main Ideas** *(page 17)*

Remind students that often the speaker will repeat the important words or main ideas many times.

E 1.13 **Listening for Details** *(page 17)*

Give students time to read the choices before listening.

AFTER LISTENING

F **Critical Thinking: Reflecting** *(page 17)*

Ideas for... **EXPANSION**

Create a Venn diagram on the board and hold a group discussion on how teenagers today and teenagers in the past are the same and different.

ANSWER KEY

LISTENING

A *(page 16)* Possible answers:

Teenagers: in school, between ages 13–19, still growing

Adults: work, over 20, often married, sometimes have children

B *(page 16)* **1.** F; **2.** T; **3.** T

C *(page 17)* **1.** b; **2.** a, e

D *(page 17)* teenager, brain, feelings

E *(page 17)* ✓ family; ✓ friends; ✓ experiences; ✓ media

F *(page 17)* Answers will vary.

SPEAKING

Ideas for... **PRESENTING PRONUNCIATION: Contractions with *Be***

1.14 Write the following sentences on the board. Explain that you will say one of the sentences and they have to hold up their fingers to indicate which number sentence you said.

A. Sentence #1: I am a teenager. #2: I'm a teenager

B. Sentence #1: It's typical pop music. #2: It is typical pop music.

C. Sentence #1: They were not typical teenagers. #2: They weren't typical teenagers.

D. Sentence #1: You aren't an adult. #2: You are not an adult.

E. Sentence #1: He is growing up with his grandparents. #2: He's growing up with his grandparents.

A 1.15 *(page 18)*

Have students repeat each sentence after you before they practice with a partner.

B *(page 18)*

Have students work with several students so they get practice with listening to different accents.

C *(page 18)*

Write the sample sentences on the board. Ask a volunteer to come up and underline the contractions with *be* in the sentences. Remind students to use contractions with *be* in their sentences.

D *(page 19)*

Model how to do the activity with a few students. Ask volunteer students to stand up and engage in the conversation with you. After asking one student one question, move on to the next volunteer and ask a different question.

E *(page 19)*

Share an idea for a few of the situations listed.

Ideas for... MULTI-LEVEL CLASSES

Lower level students can write their conversation for their role-play. Expect the higher level students to role-play their situation without using notes, or at least not looking at their scripts.

Ideas for... EXPANSION

If there is time in class, or as homework, have students search for how other cultures get someone's attention in each of the situations listed in the student book (a teacher in class; a waiter in a restaurant; a friend in a store; a stranger on the street). Students share their ideas with the class.

ANSWER KEY

SPEAKING

A *(page 18)*

1. b. I'm not shy.
2. a. It is typical to feel that way.
3. b. He isn't a teenager. He's an adult.
4. a. She is a child. She is six years old.
5. b. We're not only brothers. We're twins.
6. b. They aren't my parents. They're my friends.

B-E *(pages 18–19)* Answers will vary.

35 MINS

FINAL TASK: GIVING A PRESENTATION ABOUT YOURSELF

A Personalizing *(page 19)*

Give your own examples of things that change your ideas or actions before breaking the class into pairs.

B *(page 20)*

Draw a circle on the board. Explain that if the whole circle equals 100%, ask what percentage you would give each part of your life. As an example, ask questions about the graph in the book, such as: What part of Jenna's life is most important to her? (Family = 40%); What part of Jenna's life is least important to her? (Media = 10%). Then create a pie chart on the board and give your own percentages as another example.

C *(page 20)*

Ask a volunteer to read aloud Jenna's presentation.

Ideas for... PRESENTING THE PRESENTATION SKILL: MAKING EYE CONTACT

Explain that eye contact is very important while giving a presentation. Read Jenna's presentation aloud (or write a presentation about yourself as an example) two times. The first time, present it without any eye contact. The second time, present it with eye contact and more engaging facial expressions. Ask the students which presentation was better and why. Explain that a great presentation can fail if the presenter doesn't make eye contact with the audience.

D *(page 20)*

Tell students to practice their presentation in front of a mirror. Remind them to use eye contact as much as possible. Teach them to say the presentation in chunks and to look up at their audience for as long as they can.

E Presenting *(page 20)*

If the class is large, consider breaking the class into small groups for the presentation.

TIP Remind students how to be a good audience during a presentation: keep phones on silent and put away, make eye contact with the presenter, and display positive body language and facial expressions that show interest, such as smiles and head nods.

ANSWER KEY

FINAL TASK

A–E *(pages 19–20)* Answers will vary.

REFLECTION

- Have students answer questions 1–2 on their own, and then discuss their answers in pairs or small groups.
- Ask students to discuss similarities and differences in their answers for questions 1–2. For question 3, have students compare answers and then write the words they are still unsure of on the board. Lead a class review of the challenging words and reteach terms as necessary.

2 LOVE YOUR JOB

ACADEMIC TRACK

Career Studies

ACADEMIC SKILLS

LISTENING	Listening for Signposts
	Making a List
SPEAKING	Using Listing Words
	Simple Present -s Form of a Verb
CRITICAL THINKING	Categorizing Information

UNIT OVERVIEW

The focus of this unit is on the aspects of a job that make people happy at work. The unit provides opportunities for students to share what is important for them in a job and learn about the types of jobs that are available in the 21st century.

- **LISTENING A Online Lecture: Who's happy at work?** This lecture discusses the various things, according to research, that make people happy at work.
- **VIDEO *Wanted: Adventure Storyteller:*** Fitz Cahall is a filmmaker, a photographer, and an adventure storyteller. In this video, Cahall explains his love for adventure and the outdoors, and how he combined these passions and ended up creating the perfect job for himself.
- **LISTENING B An Interview about 21st Century Jobs:** In an interview, a career advisor gives information about new jobs in the 21st Century and advice for creating the perfect job.

For the final task, students draw upon what they have learned in the unit to give a presentation about their dream job. They begin with answering questions about themselves and taking a survey to help narrow down their interests, and then from that information they think of an existing job or create their own job. Students prepare a presentation, practice it with a partner, and deliver it in front of the class.

For additional information about the topics in this unit, here are some suggestions for online search terms: *engineering jobs, stress management, work and happiness, job satisfaction, adventure storyteller, Fitz Cahall, National Geographic Adventurer of the Year, career advice, Mundano, app designer, social media manager, Walt Disney, J.K. Rowling, Thomas Edison*

20 MINS

UNIT OPENER

THINK AND DISCUSS *(page 21)*

Direct students' attention to the photo and caption. Ask guiding questions, such as:

- What are these men holding? *(a model of an airplane)*
- What do they use the model for? (*They use it to study airplanes and how they work.)*
- What is their job or occupation? (*They are engineers.*)
- Do they look happy? *(Yes, they are smiling and look happy.)*
- Why do you think engineers are happy with their work? *(Possible answer: They get to make things and use their hands. They don't have to sit at a desk all day.)*

ANSWER KEY

THINK AND DISCUSS *(page 21)*

1. Possible answers: They work with airplanes in some way. They're engineers.
2. Possible answer: They need to study math and science.
3. Answers will vary.

EXPLORE THE THEME *(pages 22–23)*

Look at the pie chart as a class, and ask students the main reason people have stress at work. (*They have too much work.*) Ask a volunteer to explain each section of the chart. Then break the class into small groups to discuss the questions. After their discussion, ask a few groups to share what they talked about.

ANSWER KEY

EXPLORE THE THEME *(pages 22–23)*

1. Possible answer: He is tired. He is probably stressed because he needs to study a lot for the college entrance exam.
2. Answers will vary.
3. Answers will vary.

Lesson A

30 MINS VOCABULARY

A 1.16 *(page 24)*
Before playing the audio, say each word aloud a few times and ask the class to repeat after you for pronunciation practice.

> Ideas for... **PRESENTATION**
> Ask students which words they already know, and have volunteers provide sample sentences to check meaning. Then give an example and a sample sentence for any word they do not know. For example, for the word *boring*, write the word on the board and say, "*Boring* means not interesting, or not fun. I never liked doing math in school. I think math is really boring." Do another example for the word *create*. Write the word on the board and say, "*Create* means to make. I like to create things out of paper. I make origami, a Japanese paper art."

B 1.17 **Meaning from Context** *(page 24)*
Tell students to look at the chart and ask them a question, such as "Do a lot of U.S. workers think their jobs are boring?" (*No, not many.*) Then tell them to look at the chart as they listen.

> Ideas for... **EXPANSION**
> Divide the class into pairs. Tell pairs to look at the chart and think of a question to ask their partner about it. Pairs take turns asking and answering questions. For example:
> A: Is a good boss important to U.S. workers?
> B: Yes, I think so. It looks like about 50% of workers think a good boss is important.

> Ideas for... **CHECKING COMPREHENSION**
> Ask questions about the information in the chart using synonyms for the vocabulary words. Encourage students to respond using the new vocabulary word. For example, ask "How many U.S. workers are happy with their job?" (*88% are satisfied with their job.*) "What percentage of workers thinks their work is fun and interesting?" (*48% of workers think their work is exciting.*) "What percentage of workers makes their own job?" (*14% create their own job.*) "What percentage of people thinks their job is not interesting?" (*2% of people think their job is boring.*)

C *(page 25)*
Review the words and definitions with the class. Ask for volunteers to provide the correct answers.

> Ideas for... **EXPANSION**
> Have students make notecards of the vocabulary words. On one side of the note card is the vocabulary word, and on the other side is the definition and a sample sentence.

D *(page 25)*
Recreate the chart on the board and elicit a few more examples of each category from the class.

> Ideas for... **EXPANSION**
> Tell students to create an antonym log in their notebook. Tell them to make a two-column list like the one on page 25 of the Student Book and to write the two entries of good/bad and adult/child in the list. Then have them add other vocabulary words that they know the antonym for (e.g., *boring/fun; satisfied/unhappy; together/alone; boss/worker; exciting/boring*) and share their list with the class.

E **Personalizing** *(page 25)*
Write the three questions on the board. Tell students to walk around the room, find a partner, and discuss the first question. After a two minutes, tell them to find a new partner and talk about the next question.

TIP Have students get up and move to find new partners. Movement can help stimulate the brain and memory.

ANSWER KEY

VOCABULARY

C *(page 25)* **1.** work; **2.** satisfied; **3.** exciting; **4.** boss; **5.** together; **6.** boring; **7.** try; **8.** create

D *(page 25)* The final two rows are possible answers.

Word	Antonym
boring	*exciting, interesting*
together	*alone*
satisfied	*unhappy*
happy	*sad*
enjoy/like	*dislike*

E *(page 25)* Answers will vary.

LISTENING: ONLINE LECTURE: WHO'S HAPPY AT WORK?

BEFORE LISTENING

A **Prior Knowledge** *(page 26)*

Ask students what they think makes people happy at work. Write their ideas on the board, including any that aren't in the list in the Student Book. Have pairs discuss their top three things that make them happy at work.

WHILE LISTENING

B 1.18 ▶ 1.3 **Listening for Main Ideas** *(page 26)*

Elicit ideas from the class on how to listen for the main idea. Review these ideas: listen for words that are repeated often; listen for what the speaker is mainly talking about.

C 1.18 *(page 26)*

Give students time to review the statements so they know what to listen for. Play the audio again if necessary. Review the answers with the class.

Ideas for... **MULTI-LEVEL CLASSES**

Play the audio again. Instruct the higher level students to write one *True/False* question related to the content. After the audio is finished, the higher level students write their questions on the board and the lower level students answer them.

Ideas for... **EXPANSION**

Have pairs or small groups research different types of jobs that relate to working with animals. (veterinarian, dog trainer, wildlife rescue worker, etc.). Students choose one job to research and give a short presentation on what that person does. Tell students to use *who, what, where, why* and *how* questions to guide their presentation. Model an example of this organizational process.

D 1.19 *(page 27)*

Give students time to review the four sentence starters before listening to the audio again.

E 1.20 **Listening for Details** *(page 27)*

Have the students share their answers with a partner first. Then elicit the answers and write them on the board.

AFTER LISTENING

F **Personalizing** *(page 27)*

Review the signpost expressions before doing the activity. Model the activity by giving your own example first.

ANSWER KEY

LISTENING

B *(page 26)* **2.** ✓ what makes people happy at work

C *(page 26)* **1.** F; **2.** T; **3.** T; **4.** F; **5.** F

D *(page 27)* **1.** helps other people; **2.** create things; **3.** thank them; **4.** happy co-workers

E *(page 27)* **1.** teachers, engineers; **2.** Possible answers: help other people, create things, a boss that thanks them, happy co-workers

F *(page 27)* Answers will vary.

SPEAKING

Ideas for... **PRESENTING GRAMMAR FOR SPEAKING:** Simple Present

Recreate the following chart on the board:

Simple Present		
facts and truths	I am a teacher. I teach students.	He is a veterinarian. He cares for animals.
schedules and routines	I work Monday through Friday. My class begins at 8:30 am.	He works at an animal hospital. He gets to the hospital at 9:00 am.
habits/ repeated events	I prepare my lessons every day. I greet my students at the door.	He checks the animals. He gives them medicine.

Talk through the three parts of the Simple Present using a *teacher* and a *veterinarian* as examples. Point out the *-s* or *-es* that gets added onto the verbs for the pronouns *he/she/it*. Elicit another job from the students and add on to the chart with the class helping you with sentence ideas.

 *(page 28)*

Ask for volunteer pairs to perform the conversation in front of the class.

B *(page 28)*

Give students time to prepare what they will say about their partner from exercise A. Encourage them to look up when they are saying their sentences.

> **Ideas for... EXPANSION**
>
> Play a guessing game with the students. Tell each student to think of a job and write two to three sentences describing what that person does for the job. Ask volunteers to say their sentences aloud and the rest of the class guesses which job it is. Encourage students to use their dictionaries to find the word in English if they don't know it. Ask the student reading the sentences to write the job on the board after the students have made their guesses. Start with an example to show the students how to do it.
>
> This person helps people in emergencies. This person puts out fires. (*Answer = a firefighter*)

C *(page 28)*

Ask volunteers to read each sentence aloud. Point out the subject in each sentence and show that when it's a third person singular subject (he/she/it) the verb takes the ending of *-s* or *-es*.

D *(page 28)*

Make five T-charts on the board. After pairs have discussed the good and bad parts of each job, ask for five volunteer pairs to come to the board and fill out the chart with the points they came up with during their discussion.

> **Ideas for... PRESENTING PRONUNCIATION: Simple Present -*s* Form of the Verb**
>
> 1.21 Write the following sentences on the board and underline the verb in each sentence.
>
> He <u>works</u> hard.
>
> She <u>needs</u> money.
>
> He <u>teaches</u> every day.
>
> Read the sentences aloud and ask the students if they hear a difference in the pronunciation of the verbs. Explain that the *-s/-es* ending sounds different in each example. Then refer students to the chart in the Student Book.

E 1.22 *(page 29)*

Have the students pair up and practice saying the list of verbs to each other.

F 1.23 *(page 29)*

Play the audio twice if necessary.

G *(page 29)*

Review how to formulate a *yes/no* question before having the students do this exercise. Write the formula on the board for students to use as a template when they ask their questions.

Does Allisa ____________________?

Yes, she ____________________ OR No, she doesn't ________________.

H *(page 29)*

Write all of the ideas on the board and then tell them that Allisa is a salesperson.

I *(page 30)*

Recreate the chart on the board. Ask volunteers to come to the board and elicit the answers from the class and write them in the chart. Have the volunteers take turns, one volunteer per job.

ANSWER KEY

SPEAKING

A *(page 28)* Answers will vary.

C *(page 28)* **1.** needs; **2.** help; **3.** takes; **4.** brings; **5.** create

D *(page 28)* Answers will vary.

E *(page 29)*

1. creates:/s/	**6.** washes: /əz/
2. reads: /z/	**7.** helps: /s/
3. fixes: /əz/	**8.** tries: /z/
4. gives: /z/	**9.** catches: /əz/
5. knows: /z/	**10.** sits: /s/

F *(page 29)* ✓ call; ✓ talk to customers; ✓ show; ✓ explain; ✓ learn; ✓ sell; ✓ help

H *(page 29)* Possible answer: salesperson or manager

I *(page 30)* Possible answers:

Web Designer	Salesperson	Engineer	Teacher
talks with people *uses a computer* *creates Web pages* *works with others* *writes*	*talks with people* *teaches* *calls customers* *uses a computer* *works with others* *explains* *sells products*	*talks with people* *uses a computer* *creates products* *works with others* *explains*	*talks with people* *teaches* *uses a computer* *creates activities* *works with others* *writes* *explains*

LESSON TASK: DISCUSSING DIFFERENT TYPES OF JOBS

A *(page 31)*

Read the jobs aloud. Ask volunteers to explain any they know about. Discuss the rest by giving examples of what each person does for each job.

B **Critical Thinking: Categorizing** *(page 31)*

Review the adjectives for each category in the chart. Ask students if they can see a vocabulary word from this unit within the word *creative* (create). Ask "If someone is *well-paid* what does that mean? Do they make a lot of money or a little money?"

C **Personalizing** *(page 31)*

Write the sample sentence on the board. Underline the word *because* and explain that this type of sentence works well when you need to explain something. Write the following conversation starter on the board so students can use it as a template when discussing their reasons with their partner.

A: Which category did you put ____________ in?

B: I put ___________________ in the ________________ category because ______________.

Ideas for... EXPANSION

During class time or as a homework assignment, have students rank (#1–#9) the jobs in exercise A according to the jobs that are the most well-paid (#1 is highest paid, #9 is lowest paid). Then have students research the typical salary for each of the jobs. (If done in class, one student could find a site online and report the answer to the class, or divide the list among the students.) Students then compare their rankings to their findings on the Internet. See which student got the most correct.

D *(page 31)*

Have students stand up and walk around the class telling three different classmates the job they chose and why.

E *(page 31)*

Be sure that the students talk to different people than they did in exercise D.

F **Critical Thinking: Interpreting** *(page 31)*

Ask each group to share what they talked about in their small group discussion.

Ideas for... MULTI-LEVEL CLASSES

Have lower level students draw a picture to illustrate the quote in exercise F. Then ask them to explain their picture to the class.

Have higher level students think of another quote that has to do with working. Ask them to share their quote with the class.

ANSWER KEY

LESSON TASK

A–F *(page 31)* Answers will vary.

Video

VIEWING: *WANTED: ADVENTURE STORYTELLER* *(page 32)*

Overview of the Video

Fitz Cahall is a filmmaker, a photographer, and an adventure storyteller. In this video, Cahall explains his love for adventure and the outdoors, and how he combined these passions and ended up creating the perfect job for himself.

BEFORE VIEWING

A *(page 32)*

Tell students to look at the photo and read the caption before discussing their thoughts with their partner.

B **Prior Knowledge** *(page 32)*

Elicit students' ideas after the pair discussion.

C *(page 32)*

Read the vocabulary words aloud and have the students repeat after you. Have students match the words to the definitions individually first, and then check them with the class.

WHILE VIEWING

D ▶ 1.4 **Understanding Main Ideas** *(page 33)*

Give students time to review the questions and answer choices before watching the video.

E ▶ 1.4 **Understanding Details** *(page 33)*

Ask volunteers to write the answers on the board so students can check their spelling.

TIP Providing students with an opportunity to do more in the class (write on the board, lead small groups, elicit answers from the class) gives students more autonomy in their learning.

AFTER VIEWING

F **Critical Thinking** *(page 33)*

Ask volunteers to share with the whole class the ideas they talked about in their small groups.

Ideas for... CHECKING COMPREHENSION

Read a list of activities aloud and ask students to stand up if that situation "makes them tick." Example activities include: sleeping outside (camping); talking to new people; playing games; swimming in the ocean; learning a new job; being in large crowded places; being alone; trying new foods, etc.

ANSWER KEY

VIDEO

B *(page 32)* Possible answers: One way to get a job is to hear about it from a friend. Another way is to read about it on the Internet. A third way is to hear it about it from a teacher. A fourth way is to hear about it from your parents.

C *(page 32)* **1.** f; **2.** d; **3.** e; **4.** a; **5.** c; **6.** b

D *(page 33)* **1.** b; **2.** d; **3.** a; **4.** c; **5.** b

E *(page 33)* **1.** job description; **2.** hire; **3.** dream; **4.** create; **5.** risks; **6.** makes you tick

F *(page 33)*

1. Possible answers: Being outside, being with his son, meeting adventurers and telling their stories, writing, making movies, National Geographic magazines
2. Answers will vary.

Lesson B

VOCABULARY

A 1.24 *(page 34)*

Ask students in pairs to discuss the words they know.

> Ideas for... **CHECKING COMPREHENSION**
>
> Check students' understanding of the vocabulary words by asking the following questions to the class:
>
> 1. Who do you get good *advice* from?
> 2. Do you or does someone you know work for a *company*?
> 3. What *companies* are in this city? (show how to make the word *company* plural)
> 4. Do you ever want to have your *own* company?
> 5. What do you do when you *fail* at something?
> 6. What *skills* do you have?

B 1.25 **Meaning from Context** *(page 34)*

After playing the audio, review the answers. Divide the class into pairs for students to practice reading the text aloud to their partner.

> Ideas for... **EXPANSION**
>
> Tell students to work in pairs to either research or think of career advice. Give time for pairs to think about it and/or do research. Then ask them to share the advice.

C *(page 35)*

Ask for volunteers to give the answers aloud. Discuss any questions.

> Ideas for... **EXPANSION**
>
> Explain that this activity will help students remember and use vocabulary words. Create a four-square chart on the board. Take one vocabulary word and model how to fill out the chart.
>
> | **Definition: skills** | **Synonym** |
> |---|---|
> | The things you are good at. | strengths |
> | **Sample Sentence** | **Examples** |
> | She has many skills. She is good at talking to people and teaching others. | talking to people, listening, working in groups, using technology, etc. |
>
> Have each student (or pair) choose one vocabulary word either from Lesson A or Lesson B of this unit (or Unit 1) and create a four-square chart for that word. Have them recreate their charts on the board and present them to the rest of the class.
>
> For multi-level classes, have the lower level students write the definition and synonym (can look in dictionary) in the chart and the higher level students write the sample sentence and examples.

D *(page 35)*

Be sure students pair up with a different partner. Ask pairs to share the ideas they discussed.

TIP Always close each activity by asking students to share what they talked about. This routine provides closure to one activity before moving on to the next.

ANSWER KEY

VOCABULARY

B *(page 34)* **1.** enjoy; **2.** advice; **3.** skills; **4.** manager; **5.** own; **6.** company; **7.** contacts; **8.** fail

C *(page 35)* **1.** d; **2.** f; **3.** e; **4.** a; **5.** g; **6.** b; **7.** c

D *(page 35)*

1. Possible answers: teachers, friends, co-workers, parents, parents' friends
2. Answers will vary.
3. Possible answers:

   Pros: more money, work with people, be in charge

   Cons: more work, more responsibility, more stress

LISTENING: AN INTERVIEW ABOUT 21ST CENTURY JOBS

BEFORE LISTENING

A **Predicting** *(page 36)*

Read the list of jobs aloud. Have pairs work together to discuss the jobs. Then go over their ideas as a class.

WHILE LISTENING

B 1.26 **Listening for Main Ideas** *(page 36)*

Give the students time to review the main idea options listed in the Student Book before playing the audio.

C 1.27 *(page 36)*

Play the audio a second time to allow students to check their answers. Review answers as a class.

> Ideas for... **EXPANSION**
>
> Point out the images of the work spaces on page 36. Give students the choice to either work alone or in pairs to come up with a drawing/sketch and plan for their ideal work space. Give certain criteria or ideas that the office space may have; for example, a work area, a relaxing/lounge area, an eating area, green space, outdoor access, etc.
>
> Students can look online or in magazines for ideas or to add pictures to their presentation. Allow time for students to work on this and then have each student/pair present their ideal work space to the class or a group.

D 1.28 **Note Taking** *(page 37)*

Ask volunteers to come to the board and write one item from the list they wrote for this exercise. Review the answers.

E 1.29 **Listening for Details** *(page 37)*

After reviewing the answers, ask about the jobs: app designer and social media manager. Discuss a possible job description for those jobs.

> Ideas for... **EXPANSION**
>
> Give students the choice to either work alone or in pairs to research a unique job and give a short presentation about it. Students research a unique job online and then give the job description to the class. Encourage students to include a picture of the job to add to their presentation.

AFTER LISTENING

F *(page 37)*

Close the exercise by reading a list of jobs aloud. Ask students to stand up if the job sounds interesting to them. Job ideas include app designer, cloud services specialist, life coach, playlist professional, sleep coach, social media manager, personal shopper, professional video-gamer, circus performer, scuba diving instructor, zookeeper, chocolate taster, food taster, golf ball diver, video game tester, travel nurse, firefighter, doctor, sports referee, English teacher.

G **Critical Thinking: Analyzing** *(page 37)*

As an alternative or an expansion, give students the option to make a list of "Pros" and "Cons" for having your own company.

ANSWER KEY

LISTENING

A *(page 36)* Answers will vary.

B *(page 36)*

2. ✓ People can create their own jobs now

3. ✓ The digital age provides opportunities for new jobs

6. ✓ People are creative and find out what people need.

C *(page 36)* **1.** create; **2.** jobs; **3.** computer, changing, creative

D *(page 37)*

1. Do what you enjoy and use the skills you have.
2. Ask the question: *What do people need?*
3. Talk to all of your contacts.
4. Just try it.

E *(page 37)* **1.** d; **2.** a; **3.** b; **4.** c

F *(page 37)*

1. Possible answers: Work first as a volunteer. You can learn more about the job and meet the people who work there. This will show the boss your work. Then when a job opens up, you will have experience and contacts there.
2. Answers will vary.

G *(page 37)* Possible answers:

Pros: can do what you love, are your own boss, get to make all of the decisions, can set your own hours

Cons: is a lot of responsibility, can be stressful, must make all of the decisions, can cost a lot of money in the beginning

SPEAKING

A *(page 38)*

Read the captions and look at the photos together as a class. Ask if anyone knows any additional information about these famous people.

> Ideas for... **EXPANSION**
>
> Have students research other people who failed at first but are now successful. Have them give a short description of the person's history.

B *(page 38)*

After the pairs discuss, tell them to make a Venn diagram to show how their ideas are the same and different. Invite a few pairs to recreate their Venn diagram on the board to present it to the class. Remind them to use the listing words from the *Speaking Skill* box as they share their partner's similarities and differences.

TIP Always give time limits for each exercise. When the students know how much time they have to do an activity, they know how much detail to provide or how deep they are expected to go into the exercise.

C *(page 39)*

Put the students in two circles: one circle inside of the other. The students in the inside circle are facing the students in the outside circle. Read the questions aloud from exercise C. Instruct the students in the two circles to align with someone in the other circle to discuss the question. After a minute, turn the lights on and off to indicate that students are to move to the next person in the circle for the next question. Then read the next question and have students discuss.

ANSWER KEY

SPEAKING

A *(page 38)* Possible answers:

1. They all failed at first, but then became very successful and famous.
2. Do not stop trying. Trying hard is important and can bring you success.

B *(page 38)* Possible answer:

Failing can be good for people. You have to fail a lot in order to make yourself or your product better.

C *(page 39)* Answers will vary.

FINAL TASK: PRESENTING YOUR DREAM JOB

A Critical Thinking: Analyzing *(page 39)*

Brainstorm with the class possible questions to use during the interview part of exercise A. For example:

1. *What is your favorite subject? Why?*
2. *What do you like to do in your free time?*
3. *What are your skills?*
4. *Do you have any contacts?*

B *(page 39)*

Review any unknown words with the class before students do this exercise individually.

C *(page 40)*

Model this exercise by giving an example for yourself.

D *(page 40)*

Have students find and circle all of the listing words and the closing phrase in the sample presentation. Remind students to add these expressions to their presentation.

E *(page 40)*

Elicit some good presentation skills and write them on the board; for example, eye contact, body language, etc. Have pairs offer feedback to each other on these skills as they practice their presentations with each other.

F Presenting *(page 40)*

If the class is large, consider breaking the class into small groups for the presentations.

TIP Remind students how to be a good audience during a presentation: keep phones on silent and put away, make eye contact with the presenter, and display positive body language and facial expressions that show interest, such as smiles and head nods.

ANSWER KEY

FINAL TASK

A–F *(pages 39–40)* Answers will vary.

REFLECTION

- Have students answer questions 1–2 and then discuss their answers in small groups.
- Ask students to discuss similarities and differences in their answers for questions 1–2. For question 3, have students compare answers and write the words they are still unsure of on the board. Review the challenging words and reteach terms as necessary.

UNUSUAL DESTINATIONS

ACADEMIC TRACK
Geography/Tourism

ACADEMIC SKILLS

LISTENING	Listening for Details
	Using a *Wh-* Question Chart
SPEAKING	Agreeing and Disagreeing
	Syllables and Stress
CRITICAL THINKING	Thinking about Pros and Cons

UNIT OVERVIEW

The focus of this unit is on unusual places to visit and travel around the world. The unit provides opportunities for students to think about their vacation preferences and discuss interesting places around the world.

- **LISTENING A** **Presentation: Unusual Southeast Asia:** In a conference presentation, a world traveler discusses less-traveled and more unusual places to visit in Southeast Asia.
- **VIDEO** ***Monkey City:*** The city of Lopburi, Thailand is home to thousands of monkeys. On one special day, the people of Lopburi hold a festival to honor the monkeys. They lay out food and drink for the monkeys, who get to feast all day on their gifts.
- **LISTENING B** **A Conversation about a Vacation:** Two friends have a conversation about an unusual vacation destination.

For the final task, students draw upon what they have learned in the unit to survey their classmates and then give a presentation on the survey results. They begin with surveying the class and creating a graph. Students then prepare a presentation about the survey results, practice it with a partner, and deliver it in front of the class.

For additional information about the topics in this unit, here are some suggestions for online search terms: *Saint Basil's Cathedral State Historical Museum, aurora borealis, Petra Jordan, Tianjin Halchang Polar Ocean World, Eqi Glacier, Indonesia, Thailand, Vietnam, Dieng Plateau, Red Lotus Lake, Bac Ha Market, Giza Pyramids, popular vacation destinations, Lopburi monkey festival, The Palm Jumelrah, ICEHOTEL*

20 MINS

UNIT OPENER

THINK AND DISCUSS *(page 41)*

Direct students' attention to the photo and caption. Ask guiding questions, such as:

- Does this look like a typical city? Explain. *(It looks different, more colorful and elaborate.)*
- What do you think about the buildings? *(They are colorful and uniquely shaped.)*
- What is a cathedral? *(It is a large or important church.)*

ANSWER KEY

THINK AND DISCUSS *(page 41)*

1. This is a photo of Saint Basil's Cathedral State Historical Museum in Russia. It is nighttime.
2. Answers will vary.
3. Answers will vary.

EXPLORE THE THEME *(pages 42–43)*

Look at the photos together. Write the words *natural* and *manmade* on the board. Discuss the meaning and ask which places in the photos are natural and which are manmade. Ask students to share a few other examples of sites around the world that are natural and manmade.

ANSWER KEY

EXPLORE THE THEME *(pages 42–43)*

Answers will vary.

Lesson A

VOCABULARY

A 1.30 *(page 44)*

Before playing the audio, say each word aloud a few times and ask the class to repeat after you for pronunciation practice.

> **Ideas for... EXPANSION**
>
> Expand the vocabulary words and review the vocabulary skill from Unit 2 by getting students to think of the antonyms of each vocabulary word. Write the following words on the board and discuss their antonyms:
>
> beautiful (*ugly*)
>
> crowded (*empty*)
>
> famous (*unknown*)
>
> quiet (*loud*)
>
> tourist (*local*)
>
> unusual (*usual*)
>
> visit (*stay*)

B 1.31 **Meaning from Context** *(page 44)*

Play the audio twice if necessary for students to complete the conversation.

> **Ideas for... MULTI-LEVEL CLASSES**
>
> Lower level students can pair up and practice the conversation between Fatima and Arturo. Ask for volunteers to perform the conversation in front of the class.
>
> Higher level students can create their own conversation about a vacation spot they know or want to visit. Encourage them to use at least five vocabulary words. Have them perform their conversations in front of the class.

C *(page 45)*

Review the words and definitions with the class. Ask for volunteers to share the meanings.

> **Ideas for... EXPANSION**
>
> Have students make notecards of the vocabulary words. On one side of the note card is the vocabulary word, and on the other side is the definition and a sample sentence. Once the notecards are made, teach students how to play games to practice the new words.

D *(page 45)*

Write the five words spread out with a line under each one on the board. After students have done the exercise, ask volunteer students to come to the board and write the synonyms under the words.

> **Ideas for... EXPANSION**
>
> Tell students to create a synonym log in an area of their notebook. (If they made the antonym log from Unit 2 in their notebooks, they can add a category for synonyms so they are all in one place.) Tell them to make a two-column list (or add a column to their antonym chart).
>
> Tell them to add the vocabulary words that they know a synonym of (visit/go to/see/stop by; beautiful/pretty; quiet/peaceful; crowded/full of people; tourist/traveler) and then share their synonym list with the class.

E **Personalizing** *(page 45)*

Have students stand up in a circle (or multiple circles if your class is large). Go around the circle asking each person to say their sentence. In order to cover the three sentences in the exercise, go around the circle three times.

TIP Varying the way in which students report back or share answers can help change the atmosphere in the classroom. Variety adds a lot to the classroom.

ANSWER KEY

VOCABULARY

B *(page 44)* **1.** famous; **2.** unusual; **3.** beautiful; **4.** crowded; **5.** visit; **6.** tourists; **7.** quiet; **8.** area

C *(page 45)* **1.** quiet; **2.** area; **3.** visit; **4.** unusual; **5.** beautiful; **6.** crowded; **7.** famous; **8.** tourist

D *(page 45)* Possible answers for the added synonyms:

1. go to, see, stop by

2. pretty, lovely, nice, attractive

3. peaceful, calm, relaxing, laid-back

4. full, packed, busy

5. traveler, visitor

E *(page 45)* Answers will vary.

LISTENING: PRESENTATION: UNUSUAL SOUTHEAST ASIA

BEFORE LISTENING

A Prior Knowledge *(page 46)*

Write the words *natural* and *manmade* on the board and ask which places in the photos are natural and which are manmade. Ask if any students have traveled to one of these countries and if they can tell something about it.

B Critical Thinking: Analyzing Visuals *(page 47)*

Remind students they need to look at the map to answer the questions. Review the answers with the class.

WHILE LISTENING

C 1.32 1.5 Listening for Main Ideas *(page 47)*

Give students time to review the statements so they know what to listen for. Review the answers with the class.

D 1.33 *(page 47)*

Write the country names on the board: Vietnam, Thailand, Indonesia. Review the answers by writing the number 1, 2, or 3 under each country name.

> **Ideas for... EXPANSION**
>
> For homework or an in-class project, have pairs or small groups work together to research one of the places in the photos on page 46 or find a different, unusual place within one of those countries. Give time for the research and parameters for the presentation. Tell students to give details on the following:
>
> What: What is the place? (Is it a manmade place? A natural place?)
>
> Why: Why should people go there?
>
> Where: Where is the place in the country?
>
> When: When is it best to visit the place?

E Listening for Details *(page 47)*

Have the students share their answers with a partner first. Then elicit the answers and write them on the board.

AFTER LISTENING

F Critical Thinking: Synthesizing *(page 47)*

To close the activity, ask small groups to share their ideas with the class.

> **Ideas for... EXPANSION**
>
> Individually or in pairs, have students think of a title of a travel book that they would write. First, they need to think of what kind of traveler they are. Do they like to go to manmade places or natural places? Do they like to go to quiet areas or crowded areas? Then have them think of a book title that relates to the type of traveling they like to do.

ANSWER KEY

LISTENING

A *(page 46)* Answers will vary.

B *(page 47)* **1.** F; **2.** T; **3.** F; **4.** F; **5.** T; **6.** T

C *(page 47)*

2. ✓ Unusual places are great to travel to.

4. ✓ Southeast Asia has a variety of unusual places.

D *(page 47)*

1. Indonesia

2. Thailand

3. Vietnam

E *(page 47)* **1.** c; **2.** a; **3.** b

F *(page 47)*

1. Possible answer: *A Different Kind of Trip* is the likely answer. She speaks of unusual places and encourages the audience to travel to unknown places. Students learned that *different* is a synonym for *unusual.*

2. Answers will vary.

SPEAKING

Ideas for... PRESENTING THE SPEAKING SKILL: Agreeing and Disagreeing

Ask a volunteer to help with the presentation of this speaking skill. Ask the student to be A in the conversation, and take the B role yourself. Emphasize the expressions for agreeing and disagreeing as you role-play the conversations.

A 1.34 *(page 48)*

Play the audio again as you review the answers. Stop it after each conversation and ask the students if the people in the conversation agree or disagree.

Ideas for... EXPANSION

Divide the students into pairs. Have pairs write a short conversation in which there is either agreement or disagreement. Tell them to use the expressions in the *Speaking Skill* box for agreeing and disagreeing. Have the pairs perform their conversations for the class.

B *(page 48)*

Monitor the exercise by walking around and making sure students are talking to all of their classmates and taking a tally of the people who agree and disagree with them.

Ideas for... EXPANSION

Have students write a question about taking a vacation. For example: *Do you like to go on vacation with friends? Do you like to go on vacation with family? Do you like to take a tour while on vacation?* Then have students walk around the room and ask their question to their classmates. Encourage them to use phrases to agree or disagree from the *Speaking Skill* box. In the end, have students report on the results of how their classmates answered the question.

Ideas for... PRESENTING GRAMMAR FOR SPEAKING: Present Continuous

Recreate the following chart on the board:

Present Continuous		
things that are happening now	I'm teaching you now. You're listening to me now.	She's looking in her book now.
ongoing activities over a period of time	They're enjoying their trip. You're not taking the tour.	He's not eating local food on his trip.

Talk through the two meanings of the present continuous using the sentences as examples. Act out the activities as you talk about the things that are happening now. Refer students to the chart on page 49 to continue with the presentation.

C 1.35 *(page 49)*

Have students complete the conversation individually and then practice it in pairs.

D **Personalizing** *(page 50)*

Be sure to point out the example in the book and review how to do the exercise. After the groups have worked together, ask a few students to share their riddle with the rest of the class.

Ideas for... EXPANSION

Ask students to find a photo of a vacation they took and tell them to bring it to class. Tell them to write their name on the back of the photo. Students then write a description of what they are doing in the photo. Lower level students can write a few simple sentences. Higher level students can write a paragraph. Instruct them to use the present continuous when describing what they are doing in the photo.

Have the students submit their descriptions. Take time to edit them and hand them back for revisions. Once students hand in a clean copy of their description, gather them all and post the photos around the room. Shuffle the descriptions and hand one to each student. The students read the description they were assigned and walk around the room looking for the photo that matches the description they have. Once they find it, they check the back of the photo to see whose photo it belongs to and finds that person. The student asks if he/she matched the right description to the right photo. If the student did match it correctly, they hand the description back to the teacher and get a new description and start the process all over again.

E *(page 50)*

Start the exercise by eliciting a few ideas for each chart together as a class.

F *(page 50)*

Monitor the group work. Make sure the students are staying on task and provide help as necessary.

TIP Make yourself available for students while they are working in small groups or doing pair work. Listen in on their conversations and discussions and take note of any language issues they may be having. If there are mistakes being made, you can review the mistakes either individually or with the whole group, depending on how widespread the issue is.

ANSWER KEY

SPEAKING

A *(page 48)*

1. Disagree; That's interesting! I don't.
2. Agree; I don't, either.
3. Agree; Me, too!
4. Disagree; Oh, really? I do.
5. Agree; I do, too.

B *(page 48)* Answers will vary.

C *(page 49)* **1.** I'm looking; **2.** I'm riding; **3.** are walking; **4.** is driving; **5.** are walking; **6.** are resting; **7.** 're smiling

D *(page 50)* Answers will vary.

E *(page 50)* Possible answers:

Typical Place

Pros: easy to get to, often cheaper, lots of hotels and restaurants

Cons: crowded, noisy, long lines waiting to see things

Unusual Place

Pros: special, real, local people are easier to talk to/may want to learn about you

Cons: difficult to get to, difficult to find a good hotel/restaurant

F *(page 50)* Answers will vary.

LESSON TASK: PLANNING A VACATION FOR YOUR TEACHER

A Critical Thinking: Analyzing *(page 51)*

Look at the photos together. Ask if anyone has ever gone to one of these places or has taken this type of vacation. Then review the adjectives in the box and model how to do the activity by choosing one adjective for one of the vacations and writing it in the chart. Then have the class continue to describe the rest of the destinations with a partner and complete the chart.

B *(page 51)*

Walk around the room as the students discuss which vacation would be best for you. Don't give anything away on which you would prefer. Just observe.

C Presenting *(page 51)*

Set time aside to have each pair present which vacation you think you would like best. Then make your choice and explain your reason for choosing that type of vacation.

Ideas for... EXPANSION

Students may choose to do the following activity individually or with a partner. Set aside time in class or assign as homework.

Students pretend to be travel agents and create an itinerary for a five-day vacation. They choose the vacation destination and research the things that can be done at that destination. Then they write up a five-day itinerary and include a price for the vacation. Students post their final itineraries along with a photo of the destination and the price around the walls of the room.

Students then go to the "vacation fair" and view all of the itineraries posted around the room. They then choose which vacation they want to take.

Close the activity by taking a vote on awards such as: Which vacation was the most popular? Which vacation was the most unusual? Which vacation was the most expensive? Which vacation was the best bargain? Which vacation was the most quiet and relaxing?

ANSWER KEY

LESSON TASK

A–C *(page 51)* Answers will vary.

Video

VIEWING: *MONKEY CITY* *(page 52)*

Overview of the Video

The city of Lopburi, Thailand is home to thousands of monkeys. On one special day, the people of Lopburi hold a festival to honor the monkeys. They lay out food and drink for the monkeys, who get to feast all day on their gifts.

BEFORE VIEWING

A Predicting *(page 52)*

Give students time to complete the chart with their ideas, and then ask students to share their ideas with the whole class. Ask if any students have any experience with monkeys. Ask these students to share their stories.

B *(page 52)*

Recreate the matching exercise on the board. Ask students to come forward and draw a line from one word to the definition. Discuss the words.

> Ideas for... **CHECKING COMPREHENSION**
>
> Check students' understanding of the vocabulary words by asking the following questions to the class:
>
> 1. What *symbols* do you know of for good luck?
> 2. What kind of *festivals* do you have in your city?

WHILE VIEWING

C ▶ 1.6 Checking Predictions *(page 53)*

Ask to see a show of hands of how many people predicted correctly in exercise A.

D ▶ 1.6 *(page 53)*

Give students time to review the questions and answer choices before playing the video again.

E ▶ 1.6 *(page 53)*

After pairs have discussed what the monkeys are doing, ask volunteers to write the present continuous sentences on the board.

AFTER VIEWING

F Personalizing *(page 53)*

G Critical Thinking: Analyzing *(page 53)*

Write a few sentence starters on the board to serve as a support for the students during their discussion.

I think it's good to have tourists because

________________.

I don't think it's good to have tourists because

______________.

TIP Providing sentence starters for students can help lower level students feel comfortable expressing their ideas. It also ensures that the students will be using correct grammatical structure during their discussion.

ANSWER KEY

VIDEO

A *(page 52)* Answers will vary.

B *(page 52)* **1.** c; **2.** e; **3.** a; **4.** b; **5.** d

C *(page 53)* Answers will vary.

D *(page 53)*

1. ✓ Bring food to the monkeys; ✓ Bring tourists to the city

2. sunglasses

3. food, water

E *(page 53)* Possible answers:

They are eating.

They are climbing.

They are stealing.

They are being naughty.

They are sitting.

They are running.

F *(page 53)* Answers will vary.

G *(page 53)* Possible answers:

Pros: bring money to town, more jobs for local people

Cons: crowded and hard to get around town, town may be dirty or have too much trash

Lesson B

VOCABULARY

30 MINS

A 1.36 *(page 54)*

Ask students to share the meaning of any words they know.

Ideas for... CHECKING COMPREHENSION

Check students' understanding of the vocabulary words by asking the following questions to the class:

3. What's a synonym of *amazing*?
4. What is on all sides of an *island*?
5. What is the opposite of *manmade*?
6. What is the *view* from our classroom window? What is the *view* from your bedroom?
7. What's the antonym of *modern*?

Ideas for... EXPANSION

If students have created an antonym and synonym log in their notebooks, have them add these new vocabulary words to their list.

B 1.37 **Meaning from Context** *(page 54)*

Discuss other places around the world that have a good mix of both manmade and natural sights; for example, the Pyramids of Giza in Egypt.

C *(page 55)*

Ask for volunteers to say the answers aloud. Discuss any questions.

Ideas for... EXPANSION

Ask for students to create word puzzles (word searches, crossword puzzles, matching games) with the vocabulary words from this unit (Lessons A and B) and any other unit from the Student Book. Students can work in pairs or do it individually. Students come to class with several copies of their puzzles and trade them with other students in the class.

D **Personalizing** *(page 55)*

Be sure students pair up with a different partner. Ask students to share the ideas they discussed.

E **Critical Thinking: Categorizing** *(page 55)*

Encourage students to research more ideas online. Recreate the chart on the board. Ask students to come to the board and write their ideas in the chart.

F *(page 55)*

Have students answer the questions in small groups or as a whole class activity.

ANSWER KEY

VOCABULARY

C *(page 55)* **1.** e; **2.** f; **3.** a; **4.** h; **5.** d; **6.** c; **7.** b; **8.** g

D–E *(page 55)* Answers will vary.

LISTENING: A CONVERSATION ABOUT A VACATION

45 MINS

BEFORE LISTENING

A **Predicting** *(page 56)*

Be sure students look at the photo and the map. Ask what students know about this area of the world.

WHILE LISTENING

B 1.38 **Listening for Main Ideas** *(page 56)*

Give the students time to review the question and answer choices before playing the audio.

Ideas for... PRESENTING THE NOTE-TAKING SKILL: Using a *Wh-* question chart

Explain that when listening there may be a time when you need to take notes. Write the *wh-* question words on the board. Review each word, explaining the type of information they would be listening for.

Who? Listen for people's names or titles.

What? Listen for the main idea.

Where? Listen for location names.

When? Listen for dates and times.

Why? Listen for reasons (the words *because* and *so*).

How? Listen for instructions or directions.

Ideas for... **EXPANSION**

Give students a little extra practice using this framework for taking notes. Read the following story aloud. Tell students to write the *wh-* words in their notebooks and to take notes on the story using the *wh-* word framework. Explain that they don't need to write full sentences—just words, dates, and short phrases.

(Story) Next month, my mother and I are taking a trip to Africa. My mother always wanted to go on a safari to see lions and elephants, so we are taking a trip to Africa. We will fly to Nairobi, Kenya, first and then take a bus to the safari area. I am so excited for our trip!

After reading the story, ask a few volunteers to come to the board and write the notes they took about the story on the board. Discuss the notes and add or delete anything as necessary. (Who? = my mother and I; What? = taking a trip; Where? = Africa / Nairobi, Kenya; When? = next month; Why? = my mother always wanted to go on a safari; How? = fly to Nairobi / bus to safari)

C 1.38 **Note Taking** *(page 57)*

Play the audio a second time to allow students to check their answers. Review answers as a class on the board.

AFTER LISTENING

D Critical Thinking: Making References *(page 57)*

Write a sentence starter on the board for students to use during their discussion. Give an example.

Sentence starter: I think this statement is true/false because ________.

Example: I think you need warm clothes inside the ICEHOTEL because the hotel is made out of ice.

ANSWER KEY

LISTENING

A *(page 56)* Answers will vary.

B *(page 56)* b.

C *(page 57)* Possible answers:

Who?	Maria is talking to Juan about her vacation.
What?	Maria went to the ICEHOTEL for her vacation.
Where?	The ICEHOTEL is in Lapland, Sweden. It is 200 km north of the Arctic Circle.
When?	Maria went to the ICEHOTEL in winter. The hotel is open from December to April.
Why?	Maria went to the ICEHOTEL because she likes to go to unusual places for her vacation.
How?	In November, builders and ice artists from around the world come together to create the hotel. They put snow onto steel walls and after the snow freezes, they take the steel walls away and the snow walls stay up.

D *(page 57)*

2. ✓ Maria likes to go to unknown places.

4. ✓ You need warm clothes inside the ICEHOTEL.

SPEAKING

Ideas for... **PRESENTING PRONUNCIATION: Syllables and Stress**

1.39 Go over the information in the box and ask students to tap out the number of syllables in each example word on their desks. To check their understanding of syllable stress, ask them to say the words aloud as they tap out the syllables again, but this time tapping slightly harder and speaking slightly louder on the stressed syllables.

A 1.40 *(page 58)*

Have students tap out the number of syllables in each target word on their desks or tables as they listen.

B *(page 58)*

Write *hotel* on the board. Ask "How many syllables does the word *hotel* have?" (*two*). Underline the syllable *tel* in the word to show the stress. Then instruct pairs to compare their answers. After pairs review, check the answers as a class. Write the words on the board and have volunteers write the number of syllables next to each word and underline the stressed syllable.

C *(page 59)*

Recreate the "Pros" and "Cons" chart on the board. Ask groups to share their ideas and write them in the chart.

ANSWER KEY

SPEAKING

A *(page 58)* **1.** 2 ho-tel; **2.** 1 love; **3.** 3 va-ca-tion; **4.** 2 spe-cial; **5.** 3 a-re-a; **6.** 3 to-ge-ther; **7.** 1 view; **8.** 3 com-pa-ny; **9.** 3 ma-na-ger; **10.** 2 fa-mous

B *(page 58)* **1.** hotel; **2.** love; **3.** vacation; **4.** special; **5.** area; **6.** together; **7.** view; **8.** company; **9.** manager; **10.** famous

C *(page 59)* Possible answers:

Pros: A guide can give you a lot of information about the places you visit. You don't have to worry about getting lost.

Cons: You are on a schedule and may have to hurry in places. You cannot do things other than what is scheduled on the tour. Sometimes other people can be difficult to travel with. You may not go exactly where you want.

FINAL TASK: PRESENTING CLASS SURVEY RESULTS

(page 59)

Think of your own question and write it on the board to serve as a model. For example: *Do you like to take a group tour or plan your own trip?* Write the following sentence starter on the board. Point it out as students write their question.

Sentence Starter: Do you like to ______________________ ____________________?

(page 60)

Model how to do this step. Tell students what your question is and make a chart on the board that relates to your question. Then walk around the class and ask your question to a few students. Each time a student responds, make a tally mark in the chart.

<table>
<tr><th>Group Tour</th><th>On Your Own</th></tr>
<tr><td>|||</td><td>𝍸</td></tr>
</table>

Instruct students to make their own chart that relates to their question in their notebook. Then have students begin their survey. Monitor the class as they walk around and survey their classmates.

(page 60)

Review the sample presentation and bar graph as a class. Use the phrases from the *Presentation Skill* box to explain the bar graph. Encourage students to use these phrases in their presentations as well.

D Critical Thinking: Interpreting *(page 60)*

Create a two-column bar graph on the board to serve as a model for students. Tell students to work in pairs to practice their presentation. Elicit some good presentation skills on the board; for example, pointing to the graph, good eye contact, memorizing chunks of the presentation, using appropriate body language, using gestures, etc.

E Presenting *(page 60)*

If the class is large, consider breaking the class into small groups for the presentations.

ANSWER KEY

FINAL TASK

A–E *(pages 59–60)* Answers will vary.

TIP Remind students how to be a good audience during a presentation: keep phones on silent and put away, make eye contact with the presenter, and display positive body language and facial expressions that show interest, such as smiles and head nods.

REFLECTION

- Have students answer questions 1–2 on their own.
- Have them discuss their answers in pairs or small groups.
- Ask students to discuss similarities and differences in their answers for questions 1–2. For question 3, have students compare their answers and then write the words they are still unsure of on the board. Lead a class review of the challenging words and reteach terms as necessary.

4 HIGH TECH, NO TECH

ACADEMIC TRACK

Technology

ACADEMIC SKILLS

LISTENING	Listening for Steps in a Process
	Using a Spider Map
SPEAKING	Giving Reasons
	Can/Can't
CRITICAL THINKING	Interpreting a Bar Graph

UNIT OVERVIEW

The focus of this unit is on the benefits and health hazards of using technology. The unit provides opportunities for students to think about how technology impacts their lives.

- **LISTENING A A Conversation about Virtual Reality:** Two friends discuss the idea of virtual reality and the benefits of using it in a classroom setting.
- **VIDEO *High Tech or No Tech?:*** What are the uses, the advantages, and the disadvantages of using technology while out in nature or at a national park? This video asks that question of today's younger generation.
- **LISTENING B Taking a Tech Break:** A class discusses the benefits for our brains and bodies when we take a break from technology.

For the final task, students draw upon what they have learned in the unit to come up with an idea for a new app. Students work with a partner and take part in a technology fair in the classroom.

For additional information about the topics in this unit, here are some suggestions for online search terms: *virtual reality, smartphones, early phones, early cameras, American National Parks, Kuri home robot, Google Glass, social media, technology in National Parks, effects of cell phone use, technology break, technology and health, Yellowstone National Park*

UNIT OPENER

THINK AND DISCUSS *(page 61)*

Go over the questions. After, ask students about their own experience with virtual reality. Ask students if they are interested in trying it (if they haven't already), and to explain why.

ANSWER KEY

THINK AND DISCUSS *(page 61)*

Possible answers:

1. The woman is using a virtual reality gaming headset.
2. She probably feels excited and amazed. She might be experiencing an adventurous sport.
3. Virtual reality is interesting to people because it allows them to see or experience things that are too expensive, far away, or scary in real life.

EXPLORE THE THEME *(pages 62–63)*

Ask for volunteers to read the dates and captions along the timeline. Then have students discuss the questions in pairs before sharing their ideas with the class.

ANSWER KEY

EXPLORE THE THEME *(pages 62–63)*

1. Possible answers: The timeline shows how telephones and cameras have changed over time. In the past, telephones were not wireless and did not have cameras or applications. Cameras used to be much larger and harder to use, and the images they produced were much lower quality. Neither cameras nor phones were common for everyone to own. Today, almost everyone has a small, thin phone that can take photos.
2. Possible answer: The television is one device that was different in the past. Television sets are still used to watch shows, but many of them now connect to the Internet.
3. Answers will vary.

Lesson A

30 MINS VOCABULARY

A 1.41 *(page 64)*

Before playing the audio, say each word aloud a few times and ask the class to repeat after you for pronunciation practice.

> Ideas for... **COMPREHENSION**
>
> Check students' understanding of the vocabulary words by asking the following questions to the class:
>
> 1. What are the *benefits* of learning English? What are the *benefits* of learning new technology?
> 2. What kind of technology *equipment* do you have at home? What *equipment* is in this classroom?
> 3. How do you *prepare* for a test? What do you do to *prepare* to come to class?
> 4. What do you *download*?
> 5. Do you think life was easier in *the past*?

B 1.42 **Meaning from Context** *(page 64)*

As a variation, have students read the text first and predict which vocabulary words go in the blanks. Then play the audio for students to check their answers.

> Ideas for... **EXPANSION**
>
> Ask students to do some research to find a tourist site that has a Virtual Reality tour. Have them report back to the class with the details they learned.

C *(page 65)*

Review the words and definitions with the class. Ask for volunteers to share the meanings.

> Ideas for... **EXPANSION**
>
> Have pairs quiz each other on the vocabulary words by taking turns saying the definition and saying the word that matches.

> Ideas for... **PRESENTING THE VOCABULARY SKILL: Adjective Order**
>
> Review the information in the box. Ask students to describe things around the classroom using two adjectives for opinion and age.

D *(page 65)*

Review the answers together as a class. Ask volunteers to read the completed sentences aloud.

E **Personalizing** *(page 65)*

Have students share a few things they talked about in their small group.

ANSWER KEY

VOCABULARY

B *(page 64)* **1.** experience; **2.** prepare; **3.** hard; **4.** download; **5.** real; **6.** the past; **7.** benefit; **8.** equipment

C *(page 65)* **1.** benefit; **2.** download; **3.** prepare; **4.** experience; **5.** real; **6.** equipment; **7.** hard; **8.** the past

D *(page 65)*

1. Virtual reality is better than boring old videos.
2. Please download this cool new app.
3. With virtual reality, you can see beautiful old things from the past.
4. This company uses some amazing modern equipment.

E *(page 65)*

1. Possible answers: The benefit of seeing something in virtual reality is that you can see it any time and you don't have to travel there. The benefit of seeing the real thing is that you can touch, smell, and feel the real thing.
2. Possible answer: Communication was better in the past. People called one another or wrote letters. That was more personal.
3. Possible answer: Technology makes our lives easier and faster. We can do more things in a shorter amount of time.
4. Answers will vary.

LISTENING: A CONVERSATION ABOUT VIRTUAL REALITY

BEFORE LISTENING

A Previewing *(page 66)*

Point out the photos on the page and ask volunteers to read the captions aloud. Elicit any personal experiences or prior knowledge students have about virtual reality headsets.

WHILE LISTENING

B 1.43 **Listening for Main Ideas** *(page 66)*

Give students time to review the statements and choices so they know what to listen for. Review the answers with the class.

> Ideas for... **PRESENTING THE LISTENING SKILL: Listening for Steps in a Process**
>
> Write the listing words on the board. Explain that these words are used to list the steps in a process or a sequence. Next, write the following steps on the board (out of order).
>
> How to do well on a vocabulary test:
>
> write the vocabulary words in your notebook
>
> write the definition for each word next to the word
>
> make flashcards of the words
>
> make flashcards of the definitions
>
> match the word flashcards with the definition flashcards
>
> practice using the words in a sentence
>
> take the test
>
> Then say the steps using the listing words (*First, Second, Then, Next*, etc.). Instruct students to listen for the listing words. Have volunteers come up and number the steps by writing #1, #2, etc. next to the steps. Point out that when ordering steps, the order of some of these words can vary; for example, *then* and *next* can be interchangeable in a sequence. Also explain that *last* and *finally* are synonyms, so they would not be used together.

C 1.44 *(page 67)*

Give students time to read the steps so they know what to listen for. Review the answers with the class.

D 1.43 **Listening for Details** *(page 67)*

Review the answers with the class.

AFTER LISTENING

E Critical Thinking: Evaluating *(page 67)*

Write students' ideas on the board.

ANSWER KEY

LISTENING

A *(page 66)* Possible answers:

The student is experiencing virtual reality. You need a headset, a phone, and headphones.

B *(page 66)* **1.** b; **2.** a; **3.** d; **4.** d

C *(page 67)* **1.** download; **2.** phone; **3.** fits; **4.** head; **5.** open; **6.** app

D *(page 67)* **1.** a; **2.** b; **3.** c; **4.** b

E *(page 67)* Possible answers:

Language learning: You can "attend" a class.

History: You can be at an event, or see a place from another time.

Math: You can test math in real situations (such as flying in space or in an airplane).

Science: You can see and feel different things (e.g., weather in the Arctic, animals, rocks on the moon, etc.).

SPEAKING

Ideas for… PRESENTING GRAMMAR FOR SPEAKING: *Can and Can't*

Write a few activities on the board such as: *play tennis, fly a plane, use a computer, use virtual reality, drive a car, speak Japanese*.

Next, ask students to make sentences using *can/can't* with these activities. As students say sentences with *can*, put a check next to the activity. As students say sentences with *can't*, put an X next to the activity. For example:

I can play tennis. ✓	I can't use virtual reality. X
I can't fly a plane. X	I can drive a car. ✓
I can use a computer. ✓	I can't speak Japanese. X

Ideas for… PRESENTING PRONUNCIATION: *Can and Can't*

1.45 After the presentation of the grammar, say the sentences from the *Ideas For…* box above again, and emphasize the pronunciation of *can/can't*.

A *(page 68)*

Write the following sentence starter on the board. Point it out and show students how to do the activity. Be sure that one student looks at page 68 and the other student looks at page 69.

Kuri can / can't ____________________.

B *(page 69)*

Monitor the exercise by walking around and making sure students are on task and researching different kinds of robots on the Internet.

Ideas for… EXPANSION

Have students research and bring in photos of a kind of robot being used today in people's homes or offices. Ask students to give a short presentation about the robot to the class.

C Critical Thinking: Analyzing *(page 69)*

Ask students if they prefer to read from a real book or an e-book and give reasons for their answer. Review the information in the *Speaking Skill* box and encourage students to use *because* and *since* when giving their reasons.

D *(page 69)*

Ask a few students to share what they talked about in their small groups. Make sure they use *because* and *since* when they give reasons for their answers.

Ideas for… MULTI-LEVEL CLASSES

Ask higher level students to create another scenario like the ones listed in exercise D. Have them share the scenario with lower level students and ask them to decide what they would do.

ANSWER KEY

SPEAKING

A *(pages 68–69)*

Partner A:

The home robot/Kuri can move around your home.

The home robot/Kuri can't wash floors.

The home robot/Kuri can read a book to you.

The home robot/Kuri can't bring things to you.

The home robot/Kuri can take pictures and video.

Partner B:

The home robot/Kuri can play music.

The home robot/Kuri can't clean your house.

The home robot/Kuri can know who is in your family.

The home robot/Kuri can't speak English

The home robot/Kuri can greet you when you come home.

B *(page 69)* Answers will vary.

C *(page 69)*

Equipment	Can	Can't
Books	*touch the book* *write in the book* *smell the book* *share the book*	*carry many books easily*
E-books	*have many books at one time* *read without a light*	*read without electricity or batteries*

D *(page 70)* Answers will vary.

LESSON TASK: PRESENTING A NEW TECH DEVICE

A Brainstorming *(page 71)*

Point out the different categories in the chart before students begin their work. Explain that planning out the technology ahead of time will make the process go much smoother.

TIP Providing time for students to brainstorm allows students to get their creative ideas flowing. Remember one rule of brainstorming is that there are no bad ideas. All ideas are valid in the beginning stages.

B *(page 71)*

Encourage students to use the sentence starters in the Student Book. Higher level students can elaborate more, but be sure that all students cover the ideas listed here.

C *(page 71)*

The vote can be anonymous or you can ask for students to vote by raising their hands. Brainstorm other categories with the class to add more awards to the exercise.

ANSWER KEY

LESSON TASK

A–C *(page 71)* Answers will vary.

Video

VIEWING: *HIGH TECH OR NO TECH?* *(page 72)*

Overview of the Video

What are the uses, the advantages, and the disadvantages of using technology while out in nature or at a national park? This video asks that question of today's younger generation.

BEFORE VIEWING

A *(page 72)*

Recreate the matching exercise on the board. Ask students to come forward and draw a line from one word to the definition. Discuss the words.

B *(page 73)*

Ask students if there are any other types of technology or social media apps they use. Encourage students to explain them to their classmates.

C Checking Predictions *(page 73)*

Ask students to share their ideas.

WHILE VIEWING

D ▶ 1.7 **Understanding Main Ideas** *(page 73)*

Give students time to review the questions and answer choices before playing the video.

E ▶ 1.7 **Understanding Details** *(page 73)*

Ask volunteers to read aloud the ways that they checked and give details from the video to explain their answers.

AFTER VIEWING

F Critical Thinking: Judging *(page 73)*

Do a few sentences together with the class to ensure students understand the task.

G *(page 73)*

Write a few sentence starters on the board to serve as a support for the students during their discussion. For example:

I think the statement ______ is for/against technology because ________________.

ANSWER KEY

VIDEO

A *(page 72)* **1.** e; **2.** d; **3.** a; **4.** b; **5.** g; **6.** c; **7.** f

B *(page 73)* Answers will vary.

C *(page 73)* Possible answers:

You can take videos or photos from high up with a drone. You can use a bird or tree app to learn about the birds and trees you see. You can use weather apps to see how the weather will be.

D *(page 73)* **1.** b; **2.** a

E *(page 73)* ✓ Instagram; ✓ Tweet; ✓ take pictures; ✓ look at trails; ✓ look at birding apps; ✓ use Google Maps to find parks

F *(page 73)* **1.** P; **2.** A; **3.** P; **4.** P; **5.** A; **6.** A

G *(page 73)* Answers will vary.

Lesson B

30 MINS

VOCABULARY

A 1.46 *(page 74)*

Read the words aloud before playing the audio. Ask students to share the meaning of any words they know.

Ideas for... CHECKING COMPREHENSION

Check students' understanding of the vocabulary words by asking the following questions to the class:

1. Are you *available* tonight?
2. Do you have to be *available* to work at any time?
3. What do you do to give your *brain* a rest?
4. Who can you always *depend on*?
5. What *effect* do you think Virtual Reality has on people?
6. Do you *worry* what technology is doing to our brains?
7. How do you stay in good *health*?

B 1.47 Meaning from Context *(page 74)*

As a variation, tell students to predict where the vocabulary words go in the text. Then play the audio and have the students check their predictions and correct any errors.

C *(page 74)*

Ask for volunteers to write the answers on the board.

Ideas for... EXPANSION

Ask students to create word puzzles (word finds, crossword puzzles, matching games) with the vocabulary words from this unit (Lessons A and B) and any other unit from the Student Book. Students can work in pairs or individually. Have students come to class with several copies of their puzzles and trade them with other students in the class.

D Critical Thinking: Inerepreting *(page 75)*

Model how to interpret and talk about the findings on the bar graph. Then, ask a few volunteer students to share some details about the graph. For example:

The graph shows that 50% of people use their cell phones to download apps.

> **Ideas for... EXPANSION**
>
> Tell students to think of a question related to the bar graph either in the *Critical Thinking* box or the graph in exercise D. Students ask their questions to the class, or in small groups.

E **Critical Thinking: Applying** *(page 75)*

Show students how to create a bar graph. Instruct them to use a piece of paper to create their own graph showing how they use their cell phone, like the one in the *Critical Thinking* box.

> **Ideas for... EXPANSION**
>
> Tell students to think of a few questions related to the bar graph they created. Post the bar graphs and questions around the room. Students walk around, look at their classmates' graphs and answer the questions about their graphs.

ANSWER KEY

VOCABULARY

B *(page 74)* **1.** health; **2.** depend on; **3.** available; **4.** hurt; **5.** brain; **6.** rest; **7.** effect; **8.** worry

C *(page 74)* **1.** hurt; **2.** effect; **3.** brain; **4.** worry; **5.** rest; **6.** available; **7.** depend on; **8.** health

D *(page 75)* **1.** 60%; **2.** text/send texts; **3.** video call; **4.** 48%; 5. text/send texts, check Internet, email

E *(page 75)* Answers will vary.

LISTENING: CLASS DISCUSSION: TAKING A TECH BREAK

BEFORE LISTENING

A *(page 76)*

Elicit a few ideas and write them on the board. Have students work individually to think of more and then discuss them with a partner.

WHILE LISTENING

B 1.48 **Listening for Main Ideas** *(page 76)*

Give the students time to review the choices before playing the audio.

C 1.48 **Listening for Details** *(page 76)*

Play the audio a second time to allow students to check their answers. Review answers as a class.

> **Ideas for... PRESENTING THE NOTE TAKING SKILL: Using a Spider Map**
>
> Recreate the spider map from the *Note-Taking Skill* box on the board. Elicit more ideas for the arms of the spider map and add the ideas to the board. Explain that spider maps start off with the big idea and then add examples or details to the branches of the map. Use the ideas below to help with eliciting ideas.

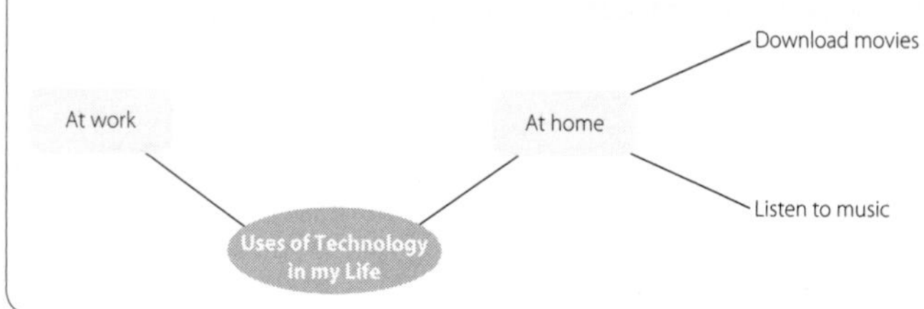

D 1.49 **Note Taking** *(page 77)*

Recreate the spider map on the board. Review the ideas in the box with the class. Have students come to the board and write the ideas they heard in the map. Then elicit any additional ideas and add them on the board.

AFTER LISTENING

E **Personalizing** *(page 77)*

To close the activity, ask the small groups to share the ideas they talked about with the whole class.

Ideas for... EXPANSION

Divide the class into two teams (or four if it is a large class). Teams will debate whether being available 24 hours a day, 7 days a week, 365 days a year is good or bad. One team will be "Pro availability" and the other team will be "Con availability." Give teams time to come up with ideas to support their side. Monitor their work.

Allow time for the teams to debate each other. Follow these debate rules:

Allow Team 1 two minutes to explain their side and give reasons.

Allow Team 2 one minute to counter Team 1's reasons.

Allow Team 2 two minutes to explain their side and give reasons.

Allow Team 1 one minute to counter Team 2's reasons.

F Critical Thinking: Synthesizing *(page 77)*

Have students recreate the map on another piece of paper so there is more space for ideas.

ANSWER KEY

LISTENING

A *(page 76)* Possible answers:

1. *The light from a phone or computer can hurt our eyes.*
2. *Sitting at a computer all day can hurt our backs since we don't sit up straight.*

B *(page 76)*

2. ✓ Using your smartphone too much can have bad effects.

3. ✓ It is good to take a break from our phones.

C *(page 76)* **1.** T; **2.** F; **3.** F; **4.** F; **5.** T; **6.** T

D *(page 77)*

1. Brain: attention problems; can't rest due to light; memory problems

2. Body: no sleep; being available 24/7/365; stress

E *(page 77)* Answers will vary.

SPEAKING

Ideas for... PRESENTING THE EVERYDAY LANGUAGE: Expressing Emotions

Explain that the Everyday Language expressions for expressing emotion are important to use when listening, and a way to reinforce the ideas is to use facial expressions.

Demonstrate how to show the following emotions (exaggerate the facial expressions to really get the idea across to the students):

- interest (raise eyebrows, lean in with body)
- surprise (open mouth, widen eyes)
- happiness (smile)
- sadness (frown)

A 1.50 *(page 78)*

Have students read the conversation before listening to the audio. Tell students to predict the expression that will be used and the emotion they express. Then play the audio and have students check their predictions. Review the answers together by having two students role-play the conversation in front of the class. Encourage the volunteers to use facial expressions and body language to express their emotions as well.

B *(page 78)*

Tell students to show the app to their partner while explaining it if possible.

TIP Using real-life tasks as practice activities in class shows the students there is a real purpose in learning a language.

C *(page 79)*

Write sentence starters on the board to help students with their explanations. Recreate the spider map on the board and model the exercise by sharing ideas from your life.

Sentence Starters:

At home/school/work/ I use technology for

__________________.

For my health/entertainment/hobby, I use technology for

__________________.

Also, remind students to use the expressions in the *Everyday Language* box to express emotion when listening to their partner.

D Personalizing *(page 79)*

After students discuss the questions with their partner from exercise D, have them find a new partner and go over the same questions for more practice. Write the following sentence starters on the board to help guide students with the discussion questions:

1. ____________ is an area of my life where I use too much/not enough technology.
2. I use my ____________ most in my life.
3. We are similar/different in ____________.
4. I want/don't want to change how I use technology in my life because ____________.

ANSWER KEY

SPEAKING

A *(page 78)*

1. How cool! Emotion: Showing interest
2. That's so interesting! Emotion: Showing interest
3. Really? Emotion: Showing surprise
4. Are you serious? Emotion: Showing surprise
5. I'm sorry to hear that. Emotion: Showing sadness

C–D *(page 79)* Answers will vary.

FINAL TASK: PRESENTING A NEW APP

A *(page 80)*

To help students generate ideas, elicit one or two examples of existing apps for each category in the box.

B Brainstorming *(page 80)*

Model how to create a spider map or *wh-* question chart on the board.

C Presenting *(page 80)*

Review the instructions on the two different roles for the pair. There are two sessions. One person stays at their "booth" and presents the app, while the other partner walks around the "fair." Then they switch roles. Be sure to give an equal amount of time for both sessions.

ANSWER KEY

FINAL TASK

A–C *(page 80)* Answers will vary.

TIP Giving students an opportunity to create something that can actually be used in real life is a motivating language learning experience.

REFLECTION

- Have students answer questions 1–2 on their own.
- Have them discuss their answers in pairs or small groups.
- Ask students to discuss similarities and differences in their answers for questions 1–2. For question 3, have students compare answers and then write the words they are still unsure of on the board. Lead a class review of the challenging words and reteach terms as necessary.

RISK AND REWARD 5

ACADEMIC TRACK

Psychology

ACADEMIC SKILLS

LISTENING	Listening for Examples
	Reviewing Your Notes
SPEAKING	Giving Examples
	Simple Past *-ed* Endings
CRITICAL THINKING	Paraphrasing

UNIT OVERVIEW

The theme of this unit is the risks people take in life and the possible rewards they receive from taking those risks.

- **LISTENING A** **Podcast: Adventurer of the Year:** In an interview, a student reporter talks about the National Geographic *Adventurer of the Year* award and the 2016 recipient Pasang Lhamu Sherpa Akita, a climber and mountain guide from Nepal.
- **VIDEO** ***Highlining Yosemite Falls:*** Dean Potter was one of the world's most famous and successful highliners. In his mind, the reward of highlining far outweighed the risk. This video highlights Dean Potter's passion for the outdoors and how highlining helped him feel a part of nature. Although the risks were great, the rewards were greater for him.
  Note: Dean Potter died in a BASE jumping accident on May 16, 2015 in Yosemite National Park, four years after this video. He was 43 years old.
- **LISTENING B** **A Conversation about Emma Stokes:** Two friends have a conversation about National Geographic Explorer Emma Stokes, who works to protect wild animals and the places they live.

For the final task, students draw upon what they have learned in the unit to tell a story about a time they took a risk and why. They use the simple past tense to tell their story.

For additional information about the topics in this unit, here are some suggestions for online search terms: *extreme sports, surfing, rock climbing, scuba diving, bungee jumping, Yosemite National Park, K2, Mount Everest, Pasang Lhamu Sherpa Akita, National Geographic Adventurer of the Year, Nepal, risk taking, skydiving, unusual foods, highlining, Yosemite Falls, Dean Potter, Madidi National Park, Nouabale-Ndoki National Park, Emma Stokes, lowland gorilla, diamondback rattlesnake*

UNIT OPENER

THINK AND DISCUSS *(page 81)*

Direct students' attention to the photo and caption. Ask guiding questions, such as:

- What are these shapes? Is there one shape that looks different from the others? What is it? *(sharks, a person/surfer)*
- Where is the photographer? What's the risk for the photographer? *(below the sharks; the photographer could get bitten by the sharks)*
- Why does this photographer want to get this photo? *(possibly to get recognition, and/or money for a great photograph)*
- Which do you think has more risk or reward? The surfer or the photographer? *(Possible answer: The photographer has more of a reward since he/she can get money for the photo.)*

ANSWER KEY

THINK AND DISCUSS *(page 81)*

1. Possible answer: The person is lying on a surfboard (or surfing). The person is in the Indian Ocean, off the coast of South Africa.
2. Possible answer: The person probably thinks it's a lot of fun!
3. Answers will vary.

EXPLORE THE THEME *(pages 82–83)*

In pairs, have students look at each photo and decide which one they would do, or, what could convince them, if anything, to do it (money, fame)? Ask pairs to share their thoughts.

Ideas for... EXPANSION

Create a bar graph on the board like the sample below. Fill it out according to your own personal opinion. Discuss the idea of risk vs. reward. Discuss each activity on the *Explore the Theme* pages and explain why you filled out your graph the way you did. For example: "I don't think I'd like rock climbing much, so I gave it a 2 for reward. I also think it can be dangerous to rock climb, so I gave it a 3 for risk on my graph. I love to scuba dive, so I gave it a 5 for reward. I don't think it's very dangerous to scuba dive, so I gave it a 1 for risk."

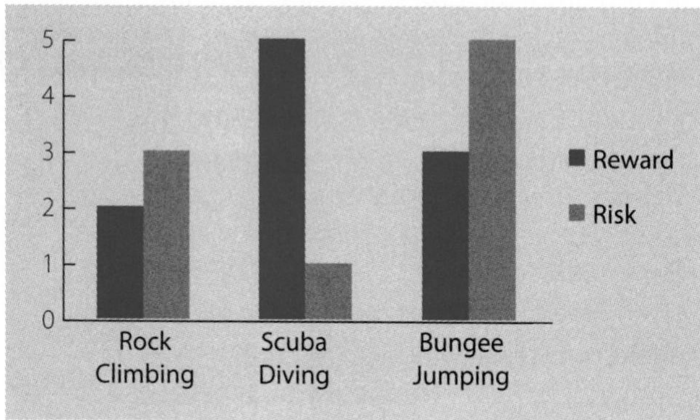

Then tell students to create their own bar graphs and explain their graph and reasoning to a partner.

ANSWER KEY

EXPLORE THE THEME *(pages 82–83)*

Possible answers:

1. Jimmy Chin is mountain climbing and taking photos, which is his job. He's a photographer for National Geographic. The person at the top is scuba diving and holding a deadly snake. The woman is bungee jumping off a bridge over a river.

   Risks for all of them are getting hurt or dying. These activities can be dangerous.
2. Many jobs are risky. Astronauts, fire fighters, and police officers take risks for their work. People like taking risks for fun, too; they drive fast cars, ride bikes in the mountains or down hills, ski and snowboard down steep mountains, and surf where there are sharks or where the waves are big and powerful.
3. People take risks because they think it is fun. They seek adventure. Some rewards are: fun, feeling good about yourself, being excited, and becoming famous.

Lesson A

VOCABULARY

A 2.2 *(page 84)*

Ask a few volunteers to share the meaning of one of the vocabulary words they know.

B 2.3 **Meaning from Context** *(page 84)*

Give students time to look over the conversations and predict which words will go in the blanks. Then play the audio and have them check their answers. Review the conversations by having volunteer students read them aloud.

Ideas for... COMPREHENSION

Help students understand and use the new vocabulary by asking questions, such as:

1. What subject do you think is *difficult* in school?
2. How old do you have to be to *vote* in your country?
3. Do you like *adventures*? Do you like the risk?
4. Do you like to *climb*? What are some things that people climb?
5. Do you play games to exercise your *mind*? What are the games?

C *(page 84)*

Review answers as a class.

Ideas for... EXPANSION

If students have created a synonym log in their notebooks, have them add the following words to their lists: adventure (*risk, unplanned event*); climb (*go up*); difficult (*hard, challenging*); mind (*brain*); solve (*answer, figure out*). Tell them to use a dictionary if necessary.

Ideas for... PRESENTING THE VOCABULARY SKILL: Noun Suffixes *-er* and *-ing*

Present the information in the box. For practice, give students two minutes to think of and list jobs that have an *-er* ending (*e.g., teacher*). When time is up, see who has listed the most jobs. Then elicit the *-er* words from the class and see how many can also take the suffix *-ing*.

D *(page 85)*

To review answers, ask volunteers to read the sentences completed with the correct words.

E *(page 85)*

To ensure that each student participates in their small group discussion, ask students to take turns leading the discussion for each question in the exercise. Alternatively, tell groups that each student must respond to each question.

TIP Giving students parameters such as how many times they have to talk in a small group encourages students who don't talk a lot to participate, and helps to minimize the amount of time the more talkative students speak.

ANSWER KEY

VOCABULARY

B *(page 84)* **1.** climb; **2.** adventure; **3.** difficult; **4.** die; **5.** body; **6.** mind; **7.** vote; **8.** solve

C *(page 84)* **1.** body; **2.** difficult; **3.** mind; **4.** solve; **5.** climb; **6.** adventure; **7.** vote; **8.** die

D *(page 85)* **1.** explorer, diver, photographer; **2.** running, swimming; **3.** player; **4.** Surfing, teacher

E *(page 85)* Answers will vary.

LISTENING: PODCAST: ADVENTURER OF THE YEAR

BEFORE LISTENING

A Previewing *(page 86)*

Remind students to look at both photos on the page and read the captions. Review the answers with the class.

WHILE LISTENING

B 2.4 ▶ 1.8 **Listening for Main Ideas** *(page 86)*

Give students time to review the statements and answer choices before playing the audio. Review the answers with the class.

C 2.5 *(page 87)*

Give students time to read the sentences before replaying the audio.

D 2.4 **Listening for Details** *(page 87)*

To review the answers with the class, ask volunteers to read each sentence with the correct word.

AFTER LISTENING

E Critical Thinking: Reflecting *(page 87)*

Have each group write their ideas on the board and present them to the class.

> **Ideas for... EXPANSION**
>
> Think of other situations similar to the situations listed in exercise E. Write them on pieces of paper and put them in a hat, bag, or cup. Students pick one situation and then give one risk and one reward for the situation they chose.

ANSWER KEY

LISTENING

A *(page 86)*

1. Nepal
2. Possible answer: She's a mountain guide, climber, and adventurer.
3. Possible answer: They do something amazing. They risk their lives.

B *(page 86)* **1.** c; **2.** b; **3.** d

C *(page 87)*

1. like; surfing
2. For example,; explorers
3. for example; climber; climb

D *(page 87)* **1.** a; **2.** b; **3.** b **4.** a; **5.** b; **6.** c

E *(page 87)* Possible answers:

- *exercising*
  risk: hurt self
  reward: look and feel great
- *going to college*
  risk: spending a lot of money, failing
  reward: learning a lot, getting a good job, helping your family
- *teaching*
  risk: long hours may be bad for health
  reward: students learn and do great things in life
- *traveling*
  risk: getting sick or hurting yourself and being far from home
  reward: seeing and learning about many different places around the world; meeting new people, trying new foods

SPEAKING

Ideas for... PRESENTING THE EVERYDAY LANGUAGE: Different Ways to Say *Yes* and *No*

Write the words *Yes* and *No* on the board in a two-column chart. Ask the students if they know other expressions that mean *yes* and *no*. Write their ideas in the correct columns on the board.

If students do not suggest the words given in the box, say some aloud (*sure, I believe so,...*) and ask students if they think the expressions mean *yes* or *no*. Write them in the correct column on the board.

A 2.6 *(page 88)*

Ask volunteers to read the conversations aloud in front of the class.

B *(page 88)*

Walk around the classroom as students are doing the exercise. Be sure they are using the expressions from the *Everyday Language* box correctly.

Ideas for... EXPANSION

Have students think of a *Yes/No* question to ask their classmates related to the theme of this unit. Then give students time to walk around the classroom asking their classmates the question. Encourage them to use the expressions from the *Everyday Language* box when responding.

C *(page 88)*

To close the exercise, ask students to share their answers to question 2 with the class.

D *(page 89)*

Be sure students are working with someone different from exercise C.

E *(page 89)*

Show how to use the scale by showing your quiz answers, adding them up, and comparing them to the scale.

F Giving Examples *(page 90)*

Have students share their opinion with the rest of the class and use the expressions in the *Speaking Skill* box to give examples to support it.

G Personalizing *(page 90)*

Ask students to share their responses to question 3: What is the most unusual food you have tried?

Ideas for... MULTI-LEVEL CLASSES

For homework, tell students to research an unusual food from around the world. Ask lower level students to choose a food, find a photo of it, and write a few sentences describing the food. Ask higher level students to choose a food, find a photo of it, and write a paragraph about it.

ANSWER KEY

SPEAKING

A *(page 88)* **1.** Of course; **2.** Absolutely; **3.** Sure; **4.** Definitely

C *(page 88)*

1. Tamas takes the most risks. Mike takes the least risks.

2. Answers will vary.

D–G *(pages 89-90)* Answers will vary.

LESSON TASK: PRESENTING A PERSONAL PLAN

A *(page 91)*

Encourage groups to come up with at least 3 ideas per category in the chart.

TIP Set expectations for the amount of work you expect for exercises. This helps students gauge how much time and effort they need to put into an exercise.

B Organizing Ideas *(page 91)*

Model an example with your own information. Ask students to complete their plan individually.

C Presenting *(page 91)*

Be sure that students work with the same group as they did in exercise A.

ANSWER KEY

LESSON TASK

A–C *(page 91)* Answers will vary.

Video

VIEWING: *HIGHLINING YOSEMITE FALLS* *(page 92)*

Overview of the Video

Dean Potter was one of the world's most famous and successful highliners. In his mind, the reward of highlining far outweighed the risk. This video highlights Dean Potter's passion for the outdoors and how highlining helped him feel a part of nature. Although the risks were great, the rewards were greater for him.

Note: Dean Potter died in a BASE jumping accident on May 16, 2015 in Yosemite National Park, four years after this video. He was 43 years old.

BEFORE VIEWING

A *(page 92)*

Be sure students look at the map and the photo when discussing the questions. Take a survey to find out who in the class would like to try this.

B *(page 93)*

Review the answers with the class. Ask volunteers to give the answers and an example of the word if possible.

WHILE VIEWING

C 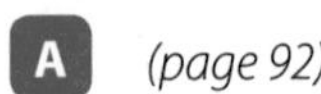 1.9 *(page 93)*

Allow time for students to read the statements before watching the video again so they know what information to focus on.

D ▶ 1.9 *(page 93)*

Review the answers by asking students to stand if the answer is true or stay seated if it's false. Elicit ways to correct the false statements.

AFTER VIEWING

E *(page 93)*

Ask small groups to share their ideas with the class.

F **Personalizing** *(page 93)*

Write the words: "Push into the unknown" on the board. Give examples of how Dean Potter does this; for example, he keeps trying even after he falls, and he continues to highline in different or more difficult places. Ask students about other people they know who push themselves. Ask students to share how they push into the unknown.

Ideas for... EXPANSION

Ask students to think how they can push themselves into the unknown—or out of their "comfort zone" on a day-to-day basis. Brainstorm ideas and then have students take a few ideas and keep a log to keep track of how they progress with pushing their limits. Some ideas for "pushing into the unknown" in class include:

- Pairing up with classmates they don't normally talk to
- Using more English in class
- Sitting in a different spot for class every day
- Being the first person to raise their hand and answer the question, or volunteering more
- Using new words they learned in class instead of using the same words they already know

Some ideas for "pushing into the unknown" outside of class include:

- Starting conversations with strangers at the bus stop, store, etc.
- Eating at a different restaurant
- Buying something that they normally wouldn't buy/wear

ANSWER KEY

VIDEO

A *(page 92)*

1. He's highlining in Yosemite during a full moon.
2. Possible answer: It's a National Park in the western United States, in the state of California.
3. Answers will vary.

B *(page 93)* **1.** c; **2.** e; **3.** a; **4.** b; **5.** d; **6.** g; **7.** f

C *(page 93)* **1.** T; **2.** T; **3.** F; **4.** T; **5.** F

D *(page 93)*

3. Dean has trouble walking the line. The wind is strong. The waterfall is noisy.

5. Dean highlines because he loves (the) beauty.

E *(page 93)* Possible answer:

It's all about being present, living in the moment, and enjoying the beauty all around you without thinking about anything else.

F *(page 93)* Answers will vary.

Lesson B

VOCABULARY

A 2.7 **Meaning from Context** *(page 94)*

After listening to the words, read them aloud and ask the class to repeat after you. Ask any volunteers to give a definition or a sample sentence for each word.

> Ideas for... **CHECKING COMPREHENSION**
>
> Check students' understanding of the vocabulary words by asking these questions:
>
> 1. What kinds of *dangers* are there in the city? In the country (natural areas)? How can you *protect* yourself from these *dangers*?
> 2. Are there any *forests* nearby? What *wild* animals do you see in the forest?
> 3. As you grow older, does your amount of free time increase or *decrease*?
> 4. Talk about something you have *discovered* lately. A new store? A new food? A new restaurant? A new activity?

B 2.8 **Meaning from Context** *(page 94)*

Have students read the article first and then listen to the audio.

> Ideas for... **EXPANSION**
>
> Write the goals people have when they risk their lives (from the article) on the board:
>
> 1. To learn
> 2. To teach
> 3. To protect
>
> Ask pairs or small groups to think of other reasons people risk their lives. For example:
>
> People risk their lives... for fun, for adventure, to find a cure for a disease, for money, for fame, etc. Have students share their ideas with the class. Write their ideas on the board. Discuss which reasons they would risk their lives for.

C *(page 94)*

Ask for volunteers to read the answers aloud. Discuss any questions students have about the vocabulary.

> Ideas for... **EXPANSION**
>
> Play a game with the students. Write words from Lesson A and Lesson B on the board. Divide the class into two teams (or more if the class is large). Give a definition for one of the words on the board. The first person in each line runs to the board and either slaps, circles, or points to the word that the definition matches. Students can confer with their teammates if they are unsure which word it is. The first person to correctly identify the word wins a point for his/her team. Continue until everyone has had one or more turns at the game.

D **Critical Thinking: Reflecting** *(page 95)*

Ask a few pairs to share what they talked about with the class.

E **Critical Thinking: Ranking** *(page 95)*

Recreate the chart on the board. Model how to do the activity by ranking the rewards according to your opinion. Then ask students to work on their own to rank the rewards.

F 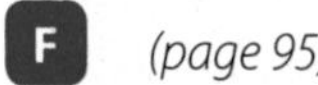 *(page 95)*

Ask a few students to come to the board and write their rankings in the chart for exercise E. Then ask them to explain their reasoning for the rankings.

ANSWER KEY

VOCABULARY

C *(page 94)* **1.** goals; **2.** count; **3.** decrease; **4.** danger; **5.** protect; **6.** wild; **7.** forest; **8.** discover

D–F *(page 95)* Answers will vary.

LISTENING: A CONVERSATION ABOUT EMMA STOKES

A Previewing *(page 96)*

Be sure students look at the map, the photos, and the information about Emma Stokes when discussing the questions.

WHILE LISTENING

B 2.9 **Listening for Main Ideas** *(page 97)*

Give students time to review the sentences and answer choices before playing the audio. Review the answers with the class.

C 2.9 **Listening for Details** *(page 97)*

Give students time to read the details before playing the audio. Review the answers with the class. Replay the audio as necessary for students to hear all of the details.

D 2.9 *(page 97)*

Ask volunteers to write the correct information from exercise C on the board.

AFTER LISTENING

E Note Taking *(page 97)*

Ideas for... **EXPANSION**

Give students time to think of something from their lives they want to share with a partner. Ideas include:

- a trip they took
- a pet they owned
- a book they read/movie they watched
- the people in their family
- a friend they have
- a funny story

Next, have students either write a paragraph about the topic they chose, or just notes on the things they want to tell. Have students tell or read their story to a partner. The partner listens and takes notes. Afterward, have pairs review their notes together to see if they covered all the details.

ANSWER KEY

LISTENING

A *(page 96)*

1. Country: Republic of the Congo
   Continent: Africa
2. Possible answer: *Endangered/At risk* means that the animal population is not strong. The animal may not exist or be alive anywhere on Earth in the future.
3. Possible answer: She hopes to protect gorillas and other animals, and to teach humans how to live with them peacefully.

B *(page 97)* **1.** b; **2.** c; **3.** c; **4.** a

C *(page 97)*

3. ✓ Emma works to protect gorillas.
4. ✓ Elephants walked through Emma's camp.
7. ✓ The number of gorillas was surprising.

D–E *(page 97)*

Possible answers:

1. Rebecca is *reading* a story.
2. Emma helps protect animals like *gorillas* in Africa and *tigers* in Asia. She protects animals in danger of dying out (not living anymore).
3. To protect the gorillas, she collects information and teaches companies and local people how to protect the land for the gorillas.
4. Emma's team was sleeping on an elephant path. The elephants walked through at night. No one was hurt. Everyone ran, and they were OK.
5. Emma and her team found *125,000* gorillas.
6. The gorillas were in a place most people didn't go. It was *not* a site for tourists, and she was the first scientist to go there. There was no path for walking. Emma and her team cut a path to walk and sometimes slept in trees.
7. No one knew that 125,000 gorillas lived there; it was a big surprise and good news, but people still need to care for the land where they live or that number can quickly change.
8. The gorilla population *is* still in danger. If a company comes in and cuts all the trees, it could hurt the gorillas. Also, a disease can quickly kill a large group of animals.

SPEAKING

Ideas for... PRESENTING GRAMMAR FOR SPEAKING: Simple Past

Write a short story or sentences about your life in the past on the board. Use at least two or three regular past verbs with *-ed*. Point to the text and ask: "Are these sentences about a time now, in the past, or in the future?" Draw a simple timeline on the board to show the meaning of past, present, and future. Ask what clues in the text show that it's in the past (*-ed* endings, words such as *past, last year, etc.*).

A 2.10 *(page 98)*

Have students try to predict which words complete the conversation. Then play the audio and have students check their answers. Ask volunteers to write the answers on the board.

Ideas for... PRESENTING PRONUNCIATION: Simple Past *-ed* Endings

2.11 Refer back to the past tense sentences on the board, or write a short new text about the past. Read the text aloud and underline each past tense verb. Ask students if they can hear a difference in the way the *-ed* forms are pronounced. Explain that the *-d/-ed* word endings have three different sounds. Refer to the Pronunciation chart in the Student Book and continue the presentation.

B 2.12 *(page 99)*

After the pair work, review the words by having a student say each word aloud. Discuss the pronunciation for each. Model the pronunciation and have students repeat as necessary.

C Personalizing *(page 99)*

Encourage students to ask their partner questions to get more information. (e.g., *Did you see it again? Was it a deadly snake? What color was it?*)

Ideas for... EXPANSION

Have students write three simple past sentences about dangers. Two are true about their lives and one is a lie. Then ask students to write their three sentences on the board or read them aloud to the class. The class guesses which is the lie.

ANSWER KEY

SPEAKING

A *(page 98)* **1.** woke up; **2.** heard; **3.** felt; **4.** didn't know; **5.** got; **6.** did, go; **7.** went; **8.** Did, find; **9.** discovered; **10.** knew

B *(page 99)*

/əd/ or /ɪd/	/t/	/d/
guided	camped	died
protected	helped	discovered
voted	jumped	received
	risked	

C *(page 99)* Answers will vary.

FINAL TASK: TELLING A STORY

A Brainstorming *(page 100)*

To provide a model for the students, tell about a time you took a risk and why.

B Organizing Ideas *(page 100)*

Recreate the chart and add in your own information to serve as a model for students.

C Presenting *(page 100)*

Remind students to ask their audience if there are any questions at the end of the presentation.

TIP Remind students how to be a good audience during a presentation: keep phones on silent and put away, make eye contact with the presenter, and display positive body language and facial expressions that show interest, such as smiles and head nods.

ANSWER KEY

FINAL TASK

A–C *(page 100)* Answers will vary.

REFLECTION

- Have students answer questions 1–2 on their own.
- Have them discuss their answers in pairs or small groups.
- Ask students to discuss similarities and differences in their answers for questions 1–2. For question 3, have students compare their answers and then write the words they are still unsure of on the board. Lead a class review of the challenging words and reteach terms as necessary.

TAKING ACTION 6

ACADEMIC TRACK
Environmental Science

ACADEMIC SKILLS

LISTENING	Listening for Emotion
	Using Symbols and Abbreviations
SPEAKING	Giving Sources of Information
	Be Going To (Gonna)
CRITICAL THINKING	Understanding Bias

UNIT OVERVIEW

This unit is about the state of our environment and things we can do to help solve many of the planet's problems. The unit provides opportunities for students to think about the impact they are making on the earth and things they can do to help alleviate some of the problems.

- **LISTENING A Student Podcast: Oceans of Plastic:** In a podcast, a student explains the problem with plastic in our oceans, citing statistics showing just how much plastic humans use and discard.
- **VIDEO *Choices:*** This two-part video makes a statement about the United States and the impact people have on the environment. Part 1 shows the beauty of the U.S., and Part 2 shows the opposite. The video is unique in that the same words are used to describe both the positive images and the negative images. The reader's tone and the images are all that differ. The message is that we must make choices about the kind of world that we want to live in.
- **LISTENING B A Conversation about Nalini Nadkarni:** Two students talk about going to hear a guest lecturer. The speaker will talk about how she increases other people's interest in trees and plants and helps the environment at the same time.

For the final task, students draw upon what they have learned in the unit to continue the project they began in the Lesson Task about solving a local problem. Students continue working with their group to add images to their project, research appropriate photos to use in their presentation, and then present it to the class.

For additional information about the topics in this unit, here are some suggestions for online search terms: *trash in oceans, how to use less plastic, recycling, plastic in oceans, Pacific garbage patch, vertical forests, Chiricahua National Monument, bias, nature in prisons, Nalini Nadkarni*

UNIT OPENER

THINK AND DISCUSS *(page 101)*

Direct students' attention to the photo and caption. Ask guiding questions, such as:

- What planet is this? *(Earth)*
- How is Earth different from other planets? (*Earth is the only planet that has an atmosphere with 21% oxygen. It is the only planet with water on its surface.*)
- Do you want to go into space?

ANSWER KEY

THINK AND DISCUSS *(page 101)*

Possible answers:

1. The weather on the Earth changes; water levels rise or fall; natural disasters, such as volcanoes and earthquakes, change the land; and people change the land.
2. Humans grow food and build things. All of these activities impact the air and land on the Earth.
3. People try to protect natural places with clean air and water laws. These laws do often change the natural places over time so they are not as dirty.

EXPLORE THE THEME *(pages 102–103)*

Point out the graph. Ask for volunteers to read about each item of trash. Ask which particular item surprised them the most.

ANSWER KEY

EXPLORE THE THEME *(pages 102–103)*

1. Possible answer:
   Trash in our oceans hurts sea creatures living there. Trash doesn't disappear quickly, and over time, the materials and chemicals from the trash affect the water.
2. Possible answers:
   It tells how long certain kinds of trash take to break down or disappear. Plastic objects are worse for the ocean because they take the longest to go away.
3. Answers will vary.

Lesson A

30 MINS VOCABULARY

A 2.13 *(page 104)*

Before playing the audio, say each word aloud a few times and ask the class to repeat after you for pronunciation practice.

Ideas for… COMPREHENSION

Check students' understanding of the vocabulary words by asking the following questions to the class:

1. What's the weather for tomorrow? (Tell students to respond with *according to* the news, the weather report, etc.)
2. Do you have any bad *habits*? What are they? Tell about some good *habits* you have.
3. How can we *reduce* the amount of trash in our classroom? How can we *reduce* the amount people use their native language during class?
4. In your opinion, what do you *believe* is the *worst* thing people can do to the planet?
5. What are some things that people *throw away* that can be recycled?

B 2.14 **Meaning from Context** *(page 104)*

As a variation, have students read the text and predict which vocabulary words go in the blanks. Then play the audio.

Ideas for… EXPANSION

Have students either work alone or with a partner. Tell students to think of another tip to use less plastic or create less trash. Give them time to brainstorm and then ask them to share their idea with the class.

Ideas for… EXPANSION

Divide students into pairs or small groups. Have them create a role-play about the reasons why it is good to stop using plastic. Give students time to write and practice the role-play. Then have them perform their role-play in front of the class.

C *(page 105)*

Review the words and definitions with the class. Ask for volunteers to give the answers.

Ideas for… EXPANSION

Have pairs quiz each other on the vocabulary words by taking turns giving the definition and the word that matches.

D *(page 105)*

Review the answers together as a class. Ask volunteers to read the completed sentences aloud.

Ideas for… EXPANSION

Write other prefixes on the board, such as *anti-; de-; fore-; bi-; super-; over-; mid-; inter-*.

Tell pairs to choose one and find three words which contain that prefix. Then have pairs write their lists on the board and teach the class the words and meanings.

E **Personalizing** *(page 105)*

Have students share a few things they talked about in their small group.

Ideas for… EXPANSION

Give students (or pairs) a big piece of paper, such as poster board or flip chart paper, and markers or colored pencils. Ask them to make a poster with tips for saving the planet (e.g., using less plastic, saving water, saving electricity, picking up trash, recycling, etc.). Give them time to make their posters and then post them around the room or throughout the hallways at the school.

ANSWER KEY

VOCABULARY

C *(page 105)* **1.** worst; **2.** especially; **3.** research; **4.** habits; **5.** according to; **6.** believe; **7.** reduce; **8.** throw away

D *(page 105)* **1.** reuse; **2.** unable; **3.** unsafe; **4.** reread; **5.** unsatisfied, redo; **6.** rewrite; **7.** unlike; **8.** recycle

E *(page 105)* Answers will vary.

LISTENING: STUDENT PODCAST: OCEANS OF PLASTIC

BEFORE LISTENING

A **Prior Knowledge** *(page 106)*

First, write the word *podcast* on the board. Ask "What is a podcast?" (*an online talk of some kind*). Be sure students look at the map and photo and their captions, as well as the title of the podcast, before talking with a partner. Ask students to share what they talked about.

B **Predicting** *(page 106)*

Read the statements together. Explain any unknown words. Don't go over the answers in this exercise. They will be revealed in the audio.

WHILE LISTENING

C 2.15 ▶ 1.10 **Listening for Main Ideas** *(page 106)*

Remind students to look at their answers in exercise B before listening to the audio or watching the slide show.

D 2.15 **Listening for Details** *(page 106)*

Give students time to review the *True/False* statements before playing the audio again. To review the answers, ask students to read the statements and share their answers and how they corrected the false statements.

E 2.16 **Note Taking** *(page 107)*

Have students write the notes with the correct symbol on the board to show the answers.

Ideas for... EXPANSION

Ask students to share one other symbol or abbreviation for note taking. Have students write it on the board with an example to share with the whole class. Start with your own example to demonstrate how to do it. For example:

Symbol for "causes" =

Trash in oceans → dead fish

Ideas for... PRESENTING THE LISTENING SKILL: Listening for Emotion

Write the following sentences on the board. Write the emotions on the board next to the sentences.

Trash is a big problem in our oceans.	passionate	sad
We need to do something about it.	passionate	sad

Ideas for... EXPANSION

Explain the difference between *passionate* and *sad.* Use your voice to demonstrate the difference by reading both sentences two times, once passionately and once sadly. Then read one with either a passionate or sad voice and have students tell the emotion that was used.

F 2.17 *(page 107)*

Ask students to share the answers aloud.

AFTER LISTENING

G *(page 107)*

Ask a few students to read it aloud so the whole class can guess which emotion they are using.

Ideas for... EXPANSION

Write a neutral sentence on the board. Have students walk around the room saying the sentence to each other with an emotion. Their classmates guess which emotion they are using.

ANSWER KEY

LISTENING

A *(page 106)* Answers will vary.

B *(page 106)* Answers will vary.

C *(page 106)* **1.** is; **2.** are; **3.** isn't; **4.** hurts; **4.** hurts

D *(page 106)* **1.** F (the Pacific Ocean); **2.** T; **3.** T; **4.** F (100,000); **5.** T; **6.** F (People need to stop using so much plastic.)

E *(page 107)*

- plastic in last 10 yrs > 1900s
- 50% plastic used, used 1 time
- average American plastic trash = 185 pounds a year
- Americans throw away 35 bil. water bottles a year
- people in world use > 1 mil. plastic bags a minute

F *(page 107)* **1.** a; **2.** b; **3.** a; **4.** a; **5.** b

G *(page 107)* Answers will vary.

SPEAKING

Ideas for... PRESENTING GRAMMAR FOR SPEAKING: Future with *Be Going To*

At the top of the board write: *be going to.* Then write the words *Predictions about Future* and *Planned Future Activity* in a two-column chart on the board. Explain that there are two meanings of the future with *be going to*. Prepare a few sentences, such as the following:

Many fish are going to die from the trash in the ocean. (Prediction about future)

I'm going to use less plastic. (Planned future activity)

They're going to clean up the park on Sunday. (Planned future activity)

It's going to rain tomorrow. (Prediction about future)

Read each sentence aloud and ask students which category the sentence falls under: *Predictions about Future* or *Planned Future Activity*. Write the sentence in the correct column.

A *(page 108)*

Ask students to share their responses and explain whether each statement is written as a prediction or a planned future activity.

Ideas for... PRESENTING PRONUNCIATION: *Be Going To (Gonna)*

2.18 Present the information in the box. For additional practice, have students read the sentences in the Grammar for Speaking chart and the sentences in exercise A. Tell them to practice pronouncing the words *going to* as *gonna*. First, have them practice on their own and then with a partner.

B *(page 108)*

Ideas for... EXPANSION

Divide the class into pairs. Tell pairs to write a conversation about how they are going to help the planet. Tell them to use the future with *be going to*. Give them time to practice it and then have them perform it in front of the class.

C 2.19 *(page 109)*

Give students time to read the options before playing the audio. Review the answers together with the class.

D 2.19 **Critical Thinking: Categorizing** *(page 109)*

Ask students to share who is going to do each item. Write the sample sentence on the board for students to use as a model: *Emily is going to read the plans discussed at last month's meeting.*

E *(page 110)*

Remind students to use the expressions in the *Speaking Skill* box when giving the source.

F **Personalizing** *(page 110)*

To model how to do the exercise, recreate the first part of the chart on the board. Go through the questions and complete one column with your personal information.

G **Critical Thinking: Analyzing Results** *(page 110)*

Write the following sentence starter on the board to use as a model when sharing the results with the class.

According to our survey, ______________________.

ANSWER KEY

SPEAKING

A *(page 108)* Answers will vary according to students' opinions.
1. are/aren't going to
2. are/aren't going to
3. is/isn't going to
4. are/aren't going to
5. am/am not going to
6. Answers will vary.

B *(page 108)* Answers will vary.

C *(page 109)* All of the actions should be checked.

D *(page 109)*
1. Emily: 1, 10
2. The group: 2, 3, 9
3. Tim: 4
4. Nanjing, China: 5
5. Vladimir: 6
6. Kumiko: 7, 8

E *(page 110)* Possible answers:
1. According to the diagram, ...
2. The podcast stated that ...
3. According to "Easy Ways You Can Use Less Plastic," ...
4. According to the Clean and Green project manager, Emily, ...

F–G *(page 110)* Answers will vary.

LESSON TASK: PRESENTING A PROJECT PLAN

A Brainstorming *(page 111)*

Brainstorm a few problems with the class first before dividing them into small groups. Divide students up into multi-level groups so that lower level students can get assistance from the higher level students if necessary.

TIP Having a real problem to solve in class can provide students with real purpose. Often students will focus so much on solving the problem that they forget they are practicing their English.

B Organizing Ideas *(page 111)*

If the groups have mixed levels, encourage students to work together to prepare the presentations and work together when practicing their parts.

C Presenting *(page 111)*

Read the sample presentation aloud so students have a model for their own presentations.

Ideas for... EXPANSION

Divide the class into pairs. Tell pairs to research volunteer opportunities in the community for helping the environment. Give students time for their research, and then ask what they found out. Ask the other students to take notes on the information their classmates give.

Close by asking if anyone plans to participate in any of the volunteer opportunities. If there is enough interest, make a plan to meet outside of class to do projects together.

ANSWER KEY

LESSON TASK

A–C *(page 111)* Answers will vary.

Video

VIEWING: *CHOICES* *(page 112)*

Overview of the Video

This two-part video makes a statement about the impact Americans have on their environment. It shows the natural and manmade beauty of the country as well as the trash, pollution, and damage that Americans have caused. The message is that we must make choices about the kind of world we want to live in.

BEFORE VIEWING

A *(page 112)*

Draw students' attention to the two photos and their captions before beginning the discussion. Ask what each photo is and how they are different from one another.

B *(page 112)*

Review the answers by saying the definition aloud and asking volunteers to say the matching word.

WHILE VIEWING

C ▶ 1.11 *(page 113)*

Have students complete the chart individually while viewing. Then recreate the chart on the board. Ask volunteers to fill in the first column of the chart with their notes on the images they saw. Discuss with the class.

D *(page 113)*

Discuss the feelings with the class. Have the same students fill in the second column of the chart with their feelings about the United States. Discuss as a class.

AFTER VIEWING

 (page 113)

Ask students to share their ideas for question 3.

ANSWER KEY

VIDEO

A *(page 112)*

1. Possible answers: The first photo shows a woman on a rock in a beautiful national park in Arizona, USA. The second photo shows a manmade housing development in Arizona, USA.
2. Possible answers: The first photo is more positive, beautiful, and interesting; the second photo looks crowded, with a lot of people and maybe noise.
3. Answers will vary.

B *(page 112)* **1.** legacy; **2.** image; **3.** generations; **4.** memories; **5.** profound; **6.** extraordinary; **7.** wonder; **8.** choice

C *(page 113)* Possible images include:

Part 1: woman on rock, pretty road, natural waterfalls, bears, beach, the Statue of Liberty, Native American women, farms, old houses, lake, mountains, canoe with woman, forest

Part 2: crowded, old cars and signs, a typical road in the USA, a trash dump, zoo animals, crowded developments, traffic, trash in water with pretty bird, ugly signs, burger and fries, empty buildings, oil spill, graffiti on sign

D *(page 113)* Answers will vary regarding feelings, but generally Part 1 should leave one feeling positive about the USA due to all the natural beauty and beautiful manmade structures, and Part 2 should leave one feeling negative due to the pollution, crowded and over-built places, trash, and so on.

E *(page 113)*

1. Answers will vary.
2. Possible answer: In Part 1, the woman is happy and sounds excited about the USA. In Part 2, her voice is quieter and sounds less excited.
3. Possible answer: One example is 'fake news,' or news stories that want you to believe certain things that are not based on facts.

Lesson B

VOCABULARY

 2.20 *(page 114)*

Read the words aloud before playing the audio. Ask students to share the meaning of any words they know.

Ideas for... CHECKING COMPREHENSION

Check students' understanding of the vocabulary words by asking the following questions to the class:

1. What kind of *behavior* is expected in the classroom? What kind of *behavior* do your parents expect of you at home?
2. Do you have a *garden*? (Or, do you want a *garden*?) What kinds of things grow in your *garden*?
3. What is your *purpose* for learning English? What is the *purpose* of cleaning up the earth?
4. Do you think there are different types of *criminals*? Can *criminals* change?
5. What do you think a room in a *prison* should have? A TV? Exercise equipment?

B 2.21 **Meaning from Context** *(page 114)*

Be sure students look at the photo and caption before doing the exercise. Then play the audio. Check the answers as a class by asking volunteers to read the text aloud.

 *(page 115)*

Ask for a volunteer to read aloud each word and its meaning.

Ideas for... EXPANSION

Ask for students to create word puzzles (word finds, crossword puzzles, matching games) with the vocabulary words from this unit (Lessons A and B) and any other unit from the Student Book. Students can work in pairs or individually. Have students bring several copies of their puzzles to class and exchange them with other students to complete.

 *(page 115)*

Have students share the answers by reading the completed sentences aloud.

E **Critical Thinking: Evaluating** *(page 115)*

Invite pairs to share some of their answers from their discussion.

Ideas for... EXPANSION

Divide the class into two teams (or four if it is a large class). Teams will debate whether prisoners should have work or some other purpose while they are in prison. One team will be "Pro work/purpose" and the other team will be "Con work/purpose." Give teams time to come up with ideas to support their side. Monitor their work. Allow time for the teams to debate each other. Follow these debate rules:

Allow Team 1 two minutes to explain their side and give reasons.

Allow Team 2 one minute to counter Team 1's reasons.

Allow Team 2 two minutes to explain their side and give reasons.

Allow Team 1 one minute to counter Team 2's reasons.

ANSWER KEY

VOCABULARY

B *(page 114)* **1.** prisons; **2.** guest; **3.** garden; **4.** increase; **5.** purpose; **6.** pretty; **7.** behavior; **8.** criminals

C *(page 115)* **1.** c; **2.** f; **3.** h; **4.** e; **5.** b; **6.** a; **7.** g; **8.** d

D *(page 115)* **1.** prisoner; **2.** reuse, repurpose; **3.** gardening; **4.** gardener

E *(page 115)* Answers will vary.

LISTENING: A CONVERSATION ABOUT NALINI NADKARNI

BEFORE LISTENING

A **Previewing** *(page 116)*

Read aloud the information about Nalini Nadkarni before students discuss the question.

WHILE LISTENING

B 2.22 **Listening for Main Ideas** *(page 116)*

Give the students time to review the main idea choices before playing the audio.

C 2.22 **Listening for Details** *(page 116)*

Play the audio a second time to allow students to check their answers. Review answers as a class.

AFTER LISTENING

D **Critical Thinking: Understanding Bias** *(page 117)*

To review, write the two sentences from the Student Book on the board. Discuss if they show bias. Underline the words that show bias.

E **Synthesizing** *(page 117)*

To close the activity, ask the small groups to share their ideas with the class.

Ideas for... EXPANSION

For homework or a class project, have pairs or individuals research other prison projects that have been successful; for example, music programs, education programs, etc.

Have students create a simple presentation reporting on the *wh-* questions (*Who? What? Where? When? Why? How?*) to the class. Encourage the class to ask questions of the presenter.

ANSWER KEY

LISTENING

A *(page 116)* Possible answer:

I think she does projects that teach about nature and the importance of caring for it.

B *(page 116)*

✓ Jamal and Claudi are both interested in going to a talk Friday evening.

✓ Nalini Nadkarni works to increase people's interest in nature.

C *(page 116)* **1.** a; **2.** c; **3.** c; **4.** a; **5.** b

D *(page 117)* Possible answer:

Student 1 shows bias because the student assumes people need something to do. Student 2 shows bias because the student thinks the prisoners shouldn't have projects because they are criminals.

E *(page 117)*

1. Possible answer: Both talk about helping the environment. The first is about taking action to change personal habits. The second is about teaching people to care more and helping people at the same time. Both help people and the environment. The first lesson is more general (all receive benefits from cleaner parks, air, water, and so on). The second lesson is more personal—helping people in prisons.
2. Answers will vary.

SPEAKING

Ideas for… PRESENTING GRAMMAR FOR SPEAKING: Future with *Will*

At the top of the board write: *will.* Then write the words *Predictions about Future* and *Unplanned Future Actions* in a two-column chart on the board. Explain that there are two meanings of the future with *will.* Prepare a few sentences, such as the following:

Many fish will die from the trash in the ocean. (Prediction about future)

I'll help you! (Unplanned future activity)

I'll make the poster for the meeting. (Unplanned future activity)

It will rain tomorrow. (Prediction about future)

Read each sentence aloud and ask students which category the sentence falls under: *Predictions about Future* or *Unplanned Future Activity.* Write the sentence in the correct column.

A *(page 118)*

Point out to students that they should make their predictions based on their own opinions.

B *(page 118)*

Write the following sentence starters on the board for students to use when asking about their partner's predictions.

A: Will ________________?

B: Yes / No. I predict ____________________.

TIP Providing sentence starters can help students use the grammatical form you want them to use in the exercise.

C *(page 119)*

Make sure the students understand each situation before dividing them into pairs. To close the activity, ask a few volunteer pairs to role-play one of the situations in front of the class.

Ideas for… EXPANSION

Have each student write a situation on a piece of paper, such as:

I need a ride to school.

I need help with my homework.

I need help fixing my computer.

Explain that students will walk around the class explaining their situation to their classmates. Tell students that they can only agree to help three people. They must say "no" politely to the others. Remind the class how to use will *to agree to help* and also how to say "no" politely.

To say "yes": Sure, I'll help you! / I'll fix your computer. / I'll do it!

To say "no": I'm sorry, I can't help you today.

ANSWER KEY

SPEAKING

A *(page 118)*

1. Possible answers: I predict English will/won't be the global language of business in the future.
2. Possible answers: I predict the prisoners will/ won't care about nature when they get out of prison.
3. Possible answers: I predict many prisons will/ won't have similar projects in the future.
4. Possible answers: I predict some prisoners will/ won't work in gardens in the future.
5. Possible answers: I predict college students will/ won't work with the prison project after they graduate.
6. Answers will vary.

C *(page 119)* Answers will vary.

35 MINS FINAL TASK: PRESENTING A PROJECT USING IMAGES

A Brainstorming *(page 119)*

Give students time to review their work from the Lesson Task on page 111 of the Student Book. Remind students that while brainstorming in their groups, they should take notes of all ideas discussed.

B *(page 119)*

Give students time in class to look for photos, or assign this part of the Final Task as homework. Read the information in the *Presentation Skill* box aloud and encourage students to keep these tips in mind as they look for photos for their presentation.

C Organizing Ideas *(page 120)*

Have students prepare their presentations digitally through slide presentation software if possible. Review the sample presentation with the class so students have a model to follow.

D Presenting *(page 120)*

Divide the class into smaller groups if the class is large. Refer students to the *Speaking Skill* box on page 110 for common phrases used to give sources of information. These may be useful when describing their photos. As a reminder, elicit from students the presentation techniques they have already learned, such as making eye contact, asking for questions, using charts/visuals, etc.

ANSWER KEY

FINAL TASK

A–D *(pages 119–120)* Answers will vary.

REFLECTION

- Have students answer questions 1–2 on their own.
- Have them discuss their answers in pairs or small groups.
- Ask students to discuss similarities and differences in their answers for questions 1–2. For question 3, have students compare their answers and then write the words they are still unsure of on the board. Lead a class review of the challenging words and reteach terms as necessary.

7 LOST AND FOUND

ACADEMIC TRACK

History/Archaeology

ACADEMIC SKILLS

LISTENING	Listening for Reasons
	Using a Timeline
SPEAKING	Saying Years Correctly
	Wh- Question Intonation
CRITICAL THINKING	Recalling Information

UNIT OVERVIEW

The theme of this unit is special things that have been lost and found, and the people who search the world for lost treasures. The unit provides opportunities for students to learn about lost treasures and also talk about treasures in their own lives.

- **LISTENING A Interview with a Treasure Hunter:** In a podcast interview, a treasure hunter talks about the reasons people like to hunt for things and gives details about an ongoing treasure hunt that a wealthy man, Forrest Fenn, has set up for the world to take part in.
- **VIDEO *Dinosaur Detective:*** The Sahara desert is not a typical place to find dinosaur fossils, but Nizar Ibrahim has been successful in finding them there. In this video, we listen to Ibrahim talk about how he has to think outside of the box in order to be successful at his job and find pieces of our planet's history.
- **LISTENING B A Guided Tour of the British Museum:** A tour guide gives a group tour of the British Museum, stopping in the gallery room with objects from ancient Persia where the guide goes into detail about the Cyrus Cylinder.

For the final task, students draw upon what they have learned in the unit to give a presentation about their life history, creating a timeline of their own life to share as a visual during the presentation.

For additional information about the topics in this unit, here are some suggestions for online search terms: *King Tutankhamun, Ramses I, ancient Egypt, looters, Fabergé eggs, Carl Fabergé, treasure hunting, treasure hunters, Forrest Fenn,* Mary Celestia, *paleontologists, paleontology, Nizar Ibrahim, spinosaurus, the British Museum, the Cyrus Cylinder*

20 MINS UNIT OPENER

THINK AND DISCUSS *(page 121)*

Direct students' attention to the photo and caption. Ask guiding questions, such as:

- Who was King Tutankhamun? What is his nickname? *(An Egyptian king who ruled for only around ten years until his death at the age of 19 in 1324 B.C.. His nickname is King Tut.)*
- Why are discoveries like this one so important? (*They help people today understand more about people in the past.)*

ANSWER KEY

THINK AND DISCUSS *(page 121)*

Possible answers:

1. An Egyptian mask (King Tut's) with a black gloved hand over its mouth.
2. They steal (take) things from people, stores, or other places.
3. Things that were lost or taken and then found again. Historical information or topics about the past.

EXPLORE THE THEME *(pages 122–123)*

Point out the map. Ask students what it shows (*the trip around the world of Ramses I's mummy*). Then point out the timeline. Ask for volunteers to read the information on the timeline. Ask volunteers to summarize the story.

ANSWER KEY

EXPLORE THE THEME *(pages 122–123)*

Possible answers:

1. Ramses I was an important leader in ancient Egypt. He ruled from 1293 B.C. until his death in 1290 B.C.
2. It traveled around the world. First, looters stole it from its tomb (or grave). Then it was in a museum in Canada, though no one knew it was Ramses I. Many years later, a museum in Atlanta, Georgia (USA) bought it. Finally, a researcher in the museum in Atlanta discovered it was Ramses I and returned it to Luxor, Egypt.
3. In a museum in Egypt. Answers will vary for the second part.

Lesson A

VOCABULARY

A 2.23 *(page 124)*

Ask a few volunteers to share the meaning of any vocabulary words they know.

Ideas for... COMPREHENSION

Help students understand and use the new vocabulary by asking questions, such as:

1. Do you prefer *gold* or silver?
2. Do you prefer *jewels* or *gold*?
3. What is something that is *missing* a lot in your house?
4. What are things that people *search* for? *(treasure, gold, jewels, shipwrecks, their keys, their shoes, etc.)*
5. Did you ever play a game of *hide* and seek, where one person *hides* and the other person looks for him/her? Which did you prefer to do? *Hide* or seek?

B 2.24 **Meaning from Context** *(page 124)*

Play the audio twice if necessary. Have students read the text aloud with a partner for pronunciation practice. Monitor pronunciation and offer feedback.

C *(page 125)*

Pair students up and have them quiz each other on the words and definitions. One student reads the definition and the other student says the word.

Ideas for... EXPANSION

Have students make notecards of the vocabulary words. On one side of the note card is the vocabulary word, and on the other side is the definition and a sample sentence.

D *(page 125)*

Recreate the chart on the board and ask volunteers to come to the board and write in the answers.

Ideas for... EXPANSION

For students who have created a vocabulary log area in their notebooks from expansion activities in previous units, tell them to add the adjective form to the words that have one. For students who haven't created a vocabulary log area, instruct them to designate an area in their notebooks for them to write their new words. Students can have columns for the word, definition, adjective form, collocations, suffix, prefix, etc. Look over their vocabulary log areas every once in a while and designate time in class for them to add new words.

Ideas for... EXPANSION

Tell students to look at the word list in exercise D and choose three of the adjective forms to use in a short paragraph. They can write something true or made-up; for example, *It's very quiet and peaceful at the beach near my house, so I often go there. I'm very lucky to live in such a beautiful place.* Have students either say their sentences aloud or write them on the board.

E **Personalizing** *(page 125)*

TIP When students are discussing in pairs or small groups, walk around and monitor their discussions. Take note of any errors or usage problems and then reteach that area to the class if necessary.

ANSWER KEY

VOCABULARY

C *(page 125)* **1.** g; **2.** c; **3.** f; **4.** h; **5.** a; **6.** e; **7.** b; **8.** d

D *(page 125)* **1.** sandy; **2.** gold/golden; **3.** mysterious; **4.** lucky; **5.** colorful; **6.** powerful; **7.** magical; **8.** peaceful

E *(page 125)* Answers will vary.

LISTENING: INTERVIEW WITH A TREASURE HUNTER

BEFORE LISTENING

A Predicting *(page 126)*

Review the meaning of any unknown words in the options.

WHILE LISTENING

B 2.25 **Listening for Main Ideas** *(page 126)*

Explain that students will look at the ideas in exercise A and indicate which one of those is the first main idea they hear and which is the second they hear. Then students write the number of the main idea from exercise A on the lines in exercise B.

Ideas for... **MULTI-LEVEL CLASS**

Ask "What is your idea of the best treasure for you? Is it money? Is it jewels? Is it chocolate?" Ask lower level students to draw a picture and write a few sentences about their ultimate treasure. Ask higher level students to draw a picture and write a more detailed paragraph or story about their treasure. Give students time to draw and write and then have them either read aloud what they wrote, or post their pictures and sentences around the room for others to see and read.

Ideas for... **EXPANSION**

Have students think of a question about treasure and treasure hunting that begins with the question word *Why*. For example: *Why are the Fabergé eggs so famous?* Then have students walk around and ask their question to their classmates. Students try their best to answer the questions using the word *because*. Students write their classmates' responses to their question. Then have students share the various reasons classmates gave as their answers.

C 2.25 **Listening for Details** *(page 127)*

Before playing the audio, remind students to listen for the words *because* or *since* to find the reason for something.

AFTER LISTENING

D Critical Thinking: Reflecting *(page 127)*

Ask students to share their responses for question 3. Tally up how many people in the class agree on each option.

Ideas for... **EXPANSION**

Discuss how Forest Fenn hid a treasure somewhere for others to find. Brainstorm with the class a list of things a person could do with a treasure. Then have each person decide which option he/she would choose if they had a treasure. To make it more interesting, make "keeping the treasure" not an option for the students to choose. Some ideas to start the discussion include the following:

1. Give the treasure away, piece by piece
2. Sell the treasure and donate the money to poor people

ANSWER KEY

LISTENING

A *(page 126)* Answers will vary.

B *(page 126)*

3. ✓ A man hides a treasure for anyone to find.
5. ✓ People like the search just as much as the treasure.

C *(page 127)* Possible Answers:

1. People think they can get rich.
2. It's exciting to search for something and then find it.
3. He was sick and thought he was dying.
4. He wanted to give people the joy of adventure.
5. He wants people to get out of their houses, go outside, and be in nature.
6. The hunt is exciting.

D *(page 127)* Answers will vary.

SPEAKING

Ideas for... PRESENTING GRAMMAR FOR SPEAKING: ***Wh-*** **Questions in the Simple Past**

Write the formula for making simple past *wh-* questions on the board:

Wh- word + *did* + subject + base verb

Write a sample sentence: What did you find?

Underline each part as you explain the formula.

- Begin with a *wh-* question word
- Use the word *did* for past questions (unless the question is about the subject, e.g., *Who went home? What came next?*)
- Add the subject (pronoun or proper noun).
- Add the verb in the base form.

A *(page 128)*

To review the answers, have volunteers write the questions on the board.

Ideas for... EXPANSION

Write 10–15 questions using *wh-* words. Scramble them and write them on the board. Cover them with a big piece of paper so the students can't see them yet. For example:

put / he / where / the / ? / did / treasure
(Where did he put the treasure?)

Divide the class into two or three teams (depending on how large the class is). The first person from each team steps up to the board. Reveal the first scrambled sentence. The students try to unscramble the sentence and write it correctly on the board. They can run back to their teammates if they need help. The first student who writes the question correctly wins a point for his/her team. Continue until everyone on the team gets a turn.

Ideas for... PRESENTING PRONUNCIATION: ***Wh-*** **Question Intonation**

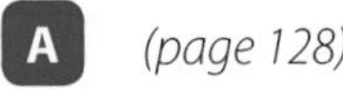 2.26 Present the information in the box. Then bring out an interesting item from your home or office. Place it in front of the room for all students to see and have students ask you *wh-* questions about it. Monitor for correct intonation as students ask their questions.

For the next day, invite students to bring in an item from their home (a souvenir from a trip, a special family item, etc.). Have students show their item to the class without explaining it. The class asks *wh-* questions to find out about it. Monitor for correct question intonation.

B *(page 128)*

Walk around the room as the pairs are working on their pronunciation. Be sure to correct any intonation patterns as necessary.

Ideas for... EXPANSION

Have students add the rising and falling arrows on the questions in the *Grammar for Speaking* box. Then have them practice pronouncing the questions with a partner.

C *(page 129)*

Encourage students to help each other remember the information without looking back at the article on page 124. To close the exercise, have volunteers write the complete questions on the board and then answer the questions.

D *(pages 129–130)*

Be sure students taking the A role in the exercise stay on page 129 and read the *Lost Treasure Ships* story. Students with the B role go immediately to page 130 and read *The Lost Ship of the Desert.*

E *(page 131)*

Model how to do the activity by reading aloud the sentences and completing the blanks with your own information. Remind students how to say *years* correctly.

ANSWER KEY

SPEAKING

A *(page 128)*

1. When you were a child, what was your favorite object?
2. As a child, where did you hide your special objects?
3. What did you search for last week?
4. When you last lost something important, what did you do?

B *(page 128)* Answers will vary.

C *(page 129)* Possible answers:

1. Q: Who was Carl Faberge?
   A: He was an artist.
2. Q: When did Alexander give his wife the first egg?
   A: In 1885.
3. Q: How often did Alexander give his wife an egg?
   A: Every year.
4. Q: How many eggs did the family have?
   A: They had 50 eggs.
5. Q: What happened to Alexander and his wife during the Russian Revolution?
   A: They were killed.
6. Q: What happened to the eggs during the Russian Revolution?
   A: Someone took them. They disappeared.
7. Q: Where are the eggs today?
   A: 43 are in museums, but 7 are still missing.
8. Q: How much are the eggs worth today?
   A: Each egg is probably worth millions of dollars today.

D *(pages 129–130)* Possible answers:

	Lost Ship of the Desert
What	Q: What did the ship do? A: It went down a river. Q: What did the ship have on it? A: Gold and jewels
Where	Q: Where did they sail? A: The Pacific Ocean, and down a river in California
When	Q: When did this happen? A: In 1615
How	Q: How did the ship go down? A: The river went dry. The ship went down in the sand.

	Lost Treasure Ships
What	Q: What did the ships do? A: They sank to the bottom of the ocean. Q: What did the ships have on them? A: Treasure
Where	Q: Where did they sail? A: From Spain to Florida. Q: Where did they sink? A: Off the coast of Florida
When	Q: When did this happen? A: In 1715
How	Q: How did the ships sink? A: They sank in a storm.

E *(page 131)* Answers will vary.

LESSON TASK: TALKING ABOUT YOUR LIFE

Ideas for... EXPANSION

Tell students to write 10 different years on a piece of paper. Then divide students into pairs. Students take turns reading their dates aloud to their partner. The partner listens and writes the dates he/she hears. Students compare the list of dates to see if both are the same.

A Brainstorming *(page 131)*

Model this step by sharing your own events. Write them on the board. Then allow time for students to think of their own important dates.

B Organizing Ideas *(page 131)*

Recreate the timeline from the Student Book on the board. Add in the important dates you shared in exercise A. Then allow time for students to write their dates and events on their timelines.

C *(page 131)*

Model this step by asking a student to help you. Tell the student one of the important dates on your timeline, and then help them formulate a *wh-* question. Continue with the other important dates on your timeline and with other students asking the questions.

D *(page 131)*

Divide the class into smaller groups if the class is large.

ANSWER KEY

LESSON TASK

A–D *(page 131)* Answers will vary.

Video

VIEWING: *DINOSAUR DETECTIVE* (page 132)

45 MINS

Overview of the Video

The Sahara desert is not a typical place to find dinosaur fossils, but Nizar Ibrahim has been successful in finding them there. In this video, we listen to Ibrahim talk about how he has to think outside of the box in order to be successful at his job and find pieces of our planet's history.

BEFORE VIEWING

 *(page 132)*

Point out the caption, the map, and the photos before students discuss the questions. Ask if they know where dinosaur fossils are typically found *(North America, China, and Argentina)*. Invite students to share any prior knowledge they have about where dinosaur fossils have been found.

 *(page 132)*

Read the words aloud before having the students match the words and definitions. Review the words as a class.

WHILE VIEWING

 1.12 *(page 133)*

Read aloud the adjectives in the box and ask students to either give a definition, a synonym, or an antonym for each.

 1.13 *(page 133)*

After reviewing the answers to this activity, ask pairs to practice explaining the events in order, using listing words such as *first, second, then*, and *next*. Ask one volunteer to tell the story to the class.

AFTER VIEWING

 **Critical Thinking: Reflecting** *(page 133)*

Ask pairs to share what they talked about for question 1.

ANSWER KEY

VIDEO

A *(page 132)*

1. He's a National Geographic Explorer. He's a paleontologist.
2. Possible answer: Dinosaur fossils (bones).
3. In the desert.

B *(page 132)* **1.** d; **2.** a; **3.** e; **4.** f; **5.** c; **6.** b

C *(page 133)* beautiful ✓; cruel ✓; frightening ✓; magical ✓; peaceful ✓

D *(page 133)*

5 The tooth gets stuck in this little sand dune in the river.
2 A dinosaur loses a tooth.
1 A dinosaur is upstream.
4 The tooth is carried downstream.
3 The tooth is rolling on the riverbed.

E *(page 133)* Possible answers:

1. I think he means that you must ask questions no one else thinks of. People thought Ibrahim was crazy because he looked for something for years, which seems crazy to many people. Answers will vary on the last question.
2. His work can help us understand life and patterns of weather and other events on the Earth.

VOCABULARY

30 MINS

A 2.27 *(page 134)*

After listening to the words, read them aloud and ask the class to repeat after you. Ask volunteers to give a definition or a sample sentence for any words they know.

> Ideas for... **CHECKING COMPREHENSION**
>
> Check students' understanding of the vocabulary words by having them discuss the following questions in small groups:
>
> 1. What *information* do you search for on the Internet every day? (*Weather, news,* etc.)
> 2. What time period in *history* do you like? Would you want to live during that time period?
> 3. What *religion(s)* are practiced in your country?
> 4. What *century* is it now?
> 5. What is included in *culture*? *(People, customs, food, holidays, the way people live,* etc.*)*
> 6. What are some *rules* of this classroom? What *rules* do you have at home?
> 7. What is the best way to keep *peace* among siblings? Among co-workers? Among countries?

B 2.28 **Meaning from Context** *(page 134)*

Review the answers by asking two students to read the completed conversation aloud. Then have pairs practice the conversation with each other, exchanging roles

C *(page 135)*

Ask for volunteers to read the answers aloud. Discuss any questions students have about the vocabulary.

> Ideas for... **EXPANSION**
>
> Play a game with the vocabulary words from this unit (Lesson A, Lesson B and the vocabulary from the Video). Write all the words on the board. Divide the class into two or three teams. Give a definition for one of the words listed on the board. The first person from each team runs to the board and "swats" the word being defined. Whoever swats the word first, wins a point for his/her team. Continue with other definitions until everyone has had at least two turns.

D *(page 135)*

If students have a vocabulary log in their notebooks, be sure to have them add these words to their log.

E **Personalizing** *(page 135)*

Be sure students pair up with a different partner.

TIP Having students work with various partners can provide more opportunities to improve listening and pronunciation skills.

> Ideas for... **EXPANSION**
>
> Students (or pairs) think of a treasure from their country and do some research about it. Give students time to write a short presentation covering the *wh-* words (*who, what, where, when, why*, and *how*). Allow time in class for students to present their treasure to the rest of the class.

ANSWER KEY

VOCABULARY

B *(page 134)* **1.** history; **2.** culture; **3.** ancient; **4.** century; **5.** rules; **6.** religion; **7.** information; **8.** peace

C *(page 135)* **1.** e; **2.** g; **3.** f; **4.** b; **5.** a; **6.** h; **7.** d; **8.** c

D *(page 135)* information – informative (or informational); religion – religious; history – historical; peace – peaceful; culture – cultural

E *(page 135)* Answers will vary.

LISTENING: A GUIDED TOUR OF THE BRITISH MUSEUM

A Previewing *(page 136)*

Ask students to share interesting ideas from their group discussion with the whole class.

> **Ideas for… EXPANSION**
>
> Discuss local museums. Elicit from the class the types of museum that are in the city they live in. Ask students if they go to any of the museums and elicit personal experiences from them. As an out-of-class assignment, ask students to choose a museum in their area and create a short report about it to present to the class. Write the following information on the board that you want students to report on:
>
> - Name of museum
> - Location (address)
> - Description of museum (Art, History, etc.)
> - Description of the items found in the museum
> - Museum hours
>
> If possible, encourage students to report about different museums, or allow them to work in pairs or groups.

WHILE LISTENING

B 2.29 Listening for Main Ideas *(page 136)*

Give students time to read the statements and answer choices before playing the audio. Review the answers with the class by having students read the completed sentences aloud.

C 2.29 Listening for Details *(page 137)*

Give students time to review the statements and answer choices before playing the audio. Review the answers with the class by having students read the completed sentences aloud.

D 2.29 Note Taking *(page 137)*

Remind students to listen for the important dates. Pause the audio as necessary for students to complete the timeline.

AFTER LISTENING

E Critical Thinking: Synthesizing *(page 137)*

Ask students to share their answers to question 1 with the class.

> **Ideas for… EXPANSION**
>
> Ask students to think of what they would do if they were the leader of their country. What changes would they make to the current rules/laws? Have students share their top three ideas. Then have students vote on who would be the best leader.

ANSWER KEY

LISTENING

A *(page 136)* Possible answers:

1. A building or place that has things from the past.
2. In London, England, U.K.
3. A very old stone with writing by someone named Cyrus. Maybe he's telling people the news or some other information.
4. The owners of the company make the rules, or the bosses and managers. Leaders do in a country. Parents at home. Teachers in a class.

B *(page 136)* **1.** a; **2.** a; **3.** b

C *(page 137)* **1.** b; **2.** c; **3.** b; **4.** b

D *(page 137)* Possible answers:

6th century B.C. (First Persian Empire); 539 B.C. (Cyrus Cylinder created); 1879 (Cyrus Cylinder found); 1880 (British Museum gets Cyrus Cylinder)

E *(page 137)* Answers will vary.

SPEAKING

A Critical Thinking: Reflecting *(page 138)*

Review the sample answers for the exercise. Give answers of your own to provide a second model before students work individually to fill in their own answers.

B *(page 138)*

Remind students of the correct intonation on *wh*-questions (rising, then falling). Also, remind students to use symbols and abbreviations when taking notes on their partner's answers. Elicit common symbols and abbreviations from the class.

C *(page 139)*

Model the activity by asking a student to read the conversation with you. Keep the conversation going as long as possible by using the phrases from the *Everyday Language* box. Then have students form groups and take turns telling about their partner's treasure. Monitor to make sure that students are keeping the conversations going using expressions from the box.

ANSWER KEY

SPEAKING

A–C *(pages 138–139)* Answers will vary.

FINAL TASK: PRESENTING A PERSONAL HISTORY

A *(page 139)*

To provide a model for the assignment, talk about one of the topics listed as it relates to your own life, listing several events to give students ideas to think about.

B Brainstorming *(page 139)*

Recreate the timeline on the board and add in the dates and events that you presented in exercise A for your own life to serve as a model. Then give students time to complete their own timelines individually.

C Organizing Ideas *(page 139)*

Ask the class to help you form sentences for the events on your timeline. Write the sentences on the board to serve as a model. Then give students time to write their own sentences.

D *(page 140)*

Read the sample presentation aloud to the students. Then read your own presentation aloud to serve as a model. Point out the time markers in the paragraph, such as *after* and *then*. Explain that these words help to join the information into a story rather than just a series of sentences.

Ideas for... PRESENTING THE PRESENTATION SKILL: Body Language

Stand in front of the class and read the sample presentation on page 140. Look down, make no facial expressions, use no hand movements, and slouch your shoulders when you read it. Ask the class for feedback on your delivery. Then read the presentation again, but with good eye contact, engaging facial expressions, hand movements, and tall, straight shoulders. Ask students to compare the two presentations and comment on which presentation looked and sounded better. Discuss the reasons.

E Presenting *(page 140)*

If the class is large, consider having students present in small groups.

TIP Remind students how to be a good audience during a presentation: keep phones on silent and put away, make eye contact with the presenter, and display positive body language and facial expressions that show interest, such as smiles and head nods.

ANSWER KEY

FINAL TASK

A–E *(pages 139–140)* Answers will vary.

REFLECTION

- Have students answer questions 1-2 on their own.
- Have them discuss their answers in pairs or small groups.
- Ask students to discuss similarities and differences in their answers for questions 1–2. For question 3, have students compare their answers and then write the words they are still unsure of on the board. Lead a class review of the challenging words and reteach terms as necessary.

8 BREAKTHROUGHS

ACADEMIC TRACK

Science/Biotechnology/Health Science

ACADEMIC SKILLS

LISTENING	Listening for Opinions
	Using a T-Chart
SPEAKING	Expressing Opinions
	Schwa /ə/ in Unstressed Syllables
CRITICAL THINKING	Considering Other Opinions

UNIT OVERVIEW

The theme of this unit is DNA research and how it relates to several areas such as extinct species, pet ownership, health, blindness, and fighting crime. The unit provides opportunities for students to think about the pros and cons of these advances.

- **LISTENING A A Class Discussion about Cloning:** Students and their professor discuss the topic of cloning in class. The professor shares information and the students ask a lot of questions.
- **VIDEO *A Chance to See Again*:** The video introduces the work of Dr. Helena Ndume from Namibia. Once a refugee, Dr. Ndume worked hard to become an eye doctor and now helps the blind in her country. She is the first recipient of the United Nations Nelson Mandela Prize.
- **LISTENING B A Lecture on Ending Blindness:** This Massive Open Online Course (MOOC) lecture gives facts about blindness and presents three treatments (cell therapy, stem cells, and bionic eyes) that may end blindness in the next 20 years.

For the final task, students draw upon what they have learned in the unit to research and plan a group presentation on one use of DNA in the real world. Students use an outline with questions to help them research, organize, and write their presentations.

For additional information about the topics in this unit, here are some suggestions for online search terms: *DNA, cells, genes, cloning,* Jurassic Park, *Dolly the sheep, saber-toothed tiger, CC the cat, Dr. Helena Ndume, United Nations Nelson Mandela prize, 3D printing, DNA testing, blindness, treating blindness, DNA phenotyping*

UNIT OPENER

THINK AND DISCUSS *(page 141)*

Direct students' attention to the photo and caption. Ask guiding questions, such as: What do you know about fingerprints? (*All are different.*) What can fingerprints be used for? (*identification; as a "password" for a phone*)

ANSWER KEY

THINK AND DISCUSS *(page 141)*

Possible answers:

1. A fingerprint at a lab. It's important because it might give information about someone who did something wrong.
2. One breakthrough is social media. It has changed the way people communicate all over the world.

EXPLORE THE THEME *(pages 142–143)*

Instruct students to read the information. Then write the following on the board (without the answers) for students to complete. Discuss the answers as a class.

DNA is like a language. Within a line of DNA you can find words, which are always 3 letters long. They make up sentences, which are called genes. Together, the genes in the DNA form instructions for the cell. An instruction might be: blue eyes, dark hair.

ANSWER KEY

EXPLORE THE THEME *(pages 142–143)*

Possible answers:

1. Cells are the smallest part of all living things. Plants, animals, and humans are made of cells.
2. DNA holds all information or instructions about different parts of plants, animals, and people. For example, it has information about hair, skin, eye color, and so on. DNA gives instructions to the cells to develop the different parts of the living thing.
3. There are many reasons scientists learn about cells and DNA, and many different ways they use the information. One example is to learn about diseases. With the information, they can find cures for diseases.

Lesson A

VOCABULARY

A 2.30 *(page 144)*

Before playing the audio, say each word aloud a few times and ask the class to repeat after you for pronunciation practice.

Ideas for... COMPREHENSION

Check students' understanding of the vocabulary words by asking the following questions to the class. Be sure to have them use the vocabulary word in their response.

1. What kind of *machines* do we have in this room? What kind of *machines* do you have at home?
2. Do you like to have the *latest* machines? The *latest* clothes? The *latest* shoes? The *latest* technology?
3. Do you buy *expensive* things? What do you spend your money on?
4. What did you want to *become* when you were young? What do you want to *become* now?

B 2.31 **Meaning from Context** *(page 144)*

Review the answers by having students read the completed sentences aloud.

Ideas for... EXPANSION

Divide students into pairs or small groups. Have them create a role-play explaining what DNA is and what it does to the cells in our body. Refer students back to the information on DNA on page 143.

Have lower level students write a short conversation using two new vocabulary words. Have higher level students write a longer role-play with at least five new vocabulary words.

Give students time to write and practice their role-plays. Then have groups perform them in front of the class.

C *(page 144)*

Review the words and definitions with the class. Ask for volunteers to share the answers.

Ideas for... EXPANSION

Have pairs quiz each other on the vocabulary words by taking turns saying the definition and the word that matches.

Ideas for... PRESENTING THE VOCABULARY SKILL: Two-Part Verbs

Write the following words on the board:

come *over*

Ask the meaning of *come*, and ask the meaning of *over*. Then write the words together on the board:

come over

Ask the meaning of this combination (*to visit*). Explain that when you put certain verbs and prepositions together, they make a two-part verb and that they have a different meaning than when the words are separated.

D *(page 145)*

Review the answers together as a class. Ask volunteers to read their example sentences aloud.

E *(page 145)*

Have students share their spider maps with a partner.

F *(page 145)*

Have one pair read the conversation aloud to check the answers with the class. Then have pairs practice the conversation, exchanging roles.

ANSWER KEY

VOCABULARY

B *(page 144)* **1.** several; **2.** copy; **3.** machine; **4.** control; **5.** expensive; **6.** become; **7.** latest; **8.** exist

C *(page 144)* **1.** copy; **2.** machine; **3.** exist; **4.** control; **5.** become; **6.** several; **7.** expensive; **8.** latest

D *(page 145)* Possible answers:

1. c (*I* ***get along*** *well with my roommates.*)
2. b (*When I* ***get back****, I'll read my emails.*)
3. d (*He* ***got off*** *the train at the wrong stop.*)
4. a (*I* ***got up*** *late this morning.*)

E *(page 145)* Possible two-part verbs:

go: go around, go away, go back, go on
break: break up, break away, break down
bring: bring up, bring back, bring on, bring over
give: give away, give up, give in
take: take away, take up, take in, take over, take on

F *(page 145)* **1.** over; **2.** back; **3.** off; **4.** from; **5.** off

LISTENING: A CLASS DISCUSSION ABOUT CLONING

BEFORE LISTENING

A Prior Knowledge *(page 146)*

Ask students to share what they talked about in their small group.

WHILE LISTENING

B 2.32 Listening for Main Ideas *(page 146)*

Give students time to read the ideas before playing the audio so they know what to listen for.

C 2.32 Listening for Details *(page 146)*

Give students time to read the True/False statements before playing the audio again. To review the answers, ask students to read the statements and share their answer.

D 2.33 *(page 147)*

Give students time to read the opinions before playing the audio so they know what to listen for.

AFTER LISTENING

Ideas for... PRESENTING THE NOTE-TAKING SKILL: Using a T-Chart

Draw a T-chart on the board. Brainstorm its uses and what kind of information could be on either side of the chart; for example:

- Pros/Cons
- Contrasting/Comparing two people, places, things, viewpoints, etc.
- Facts/Opinions
- Advantages/Disadvantages

Choose two students (or two cities, two animals, etc.) and create a T-chart for them. With the class, discuss things that can go in the two categories.

Ideas for... EXPANSION

Discuss the idea that everyone has a different fingerprint. Divide the class into pairs and tell them to discuss the pros and cons of using fingerprint identification for everyday use (getting into a phone, using a computer, getting into your bank account, entering your home, etc.). Then ask pairs to form a group of four with another pair and take notes on their ideas. Have students share their ideas by writing the pros and cons on a T-chart on the board.

E 2.33 Note Taking *(page 147)*

Recreate the T-chart for cloning animals on the board while students complete theirs individually in their books.

F *(page 147)*

Invite students to share their answers and complete the "Pro/Con" chart on the board.

ANSWER KEY

LISTENING

A *(page 146)* Answers will vary.

B *(page 146)*

2. ✓ The class is about cloning extinct animals.

4. ✓ Cloning animals may have good and bad points.

C *(page 146)* **1.** T; **2.** F; **3.** F; **4.** T; **5.** F; **6.** T

D *(page 147)* **1.** I don't think (Against); **2.** I think (For); **3.** I'm not sure (Against); **4.** I don't think (Against)

E *(page 147)*

Pros (a good idea)	**Cons** (not a good idea)
-help animal in danger of becoming extinct	*-not natural; died for reason; might hurt people* *-expensive to clone* *-problems when try to control nature*

SPEAKING

Ideas for… PRESENTING GRAMMAR FOR SPEAKING: Modals of Possibility: *Could, May, Might,* and *Will*

At the top of the board write: *could, may, might, will.* Say: Some old friends are coming over next weekend. I haven't seen them in a long time so I am not sure what they will want to do. Can you help me think of places I could take them? Start off by saying the following sentences: I **could** take them to the park. They **might** like to go to a museum. They **may** want to just stay at my house.

Each time you say a modal in the sentence, point to that modal at the top of the board. Write the following sentence starters on the board and then elicit other ideas.

You could ______________________.

They may ______________________.

They might ______________________.

After a few more ideas, say: *Well, whatever we do, I know we* ***will*** *have a good time!*

Explain that the use of *could, might,* and *may* are for events that you are not sure about. *Will* is for events that you are sure about.

Ideas for… EXPANSION

Write the following topics on the board: *Creating your Own Job, Plastic in the Oceans, Taking Risks at Work or School, Doing Extreme Sports* (e.g., highlining), *Finding Treasures, Helping Prisoners,* or your own ideas.

Ask "Do you have ideas about these topics that you are sure about? Do you have ideas that you are not sure about?" Tell students to share their ideas about the topics with a small group using *could, may (not), might (not), will (not).* For example: *Taking risks at work could help your career. You won't be happy if you don't take risks.*

A 2.34 *(page 148)*

To review the answers, have students read the paragraphs aloud.

B *(page 149)*

After pairs have worked together, tell them to switch partners with another pair and share their opinions with their new partner.

C *(page 149)*

Encourage students to use *could, may, might,* or *will* when sharing their ideas with the class. Rephrase or repeat any ideas that might benefit with an added modal.

D 2.35 *(page 150)*

Have students review the answers with the class. Write the following sentence starters on the board to help them structure their answers. Model how to say the answer for question 1 so students know how to proceed.

____________ *(Lara, Andy) has the opinion that* ______________________.

____________ *(Lara, Andy) thinks (that)* ______________________.

E 2.35 *(page 150)*

Remind students to look at the expressions in the *Speaking Skill* box when listening to the audio again. Ask which other expressions were used in the conversation.

F *(page 150)*

Tell students to use the expressions from the *Speaking Skill* box to express their opinions and the *Everyday Language* box to agree or disagree with their partner. Ask a volunteer pair to role-play their conversation for each of the statements in exercise D in front of the class.

Ideas for… EXPANSION

Have the class discuss two or three topics in the news that people don't agree on. Then divide the class into small groups to share their opinions. Remind students to use the expressions from the *Speaking Skill* and the *Everyday Language* boxes and to be polite and respectful in their discussions.

Ask the groups to share a few ideas they talked about. Create a T-chart to write their notes on the board.

ANSWER KEY

SPEAKING

A *(page 148)* Possible answers:

1. could; **2.** might; **3.** could; **4.** may not; **5.** won't; **6.** could; **7.** won't; **8.** may

B–C *(page 149)* Possible answers:

1. I don't think it's OK. It could hurt the clone mother. Also, there are many cats looking for a home now.

2. I think a person can spend his or her money how he or she wants.

3. I'm not sure it's smart to bring animals back that are very dangerous. What will they eat?

4. I love science-fiction movies! They give us ideas about the future.

D *(page 150)* **1.** Lara and Andy; **2.** Lara; **3.** Lara; **4.** Andy; **5.** Lara; **6.** Lara; **7.** Andy; **8.** Lara

E *(page 150)* The expression used the most is *I think* ...

The following expressions are also used:

1. Lara: *I'm not sure* it's a good idea.

2. Andy: *I think* it's interesting.

3. Lara: *I think* it's scary!

4. Andy: ... *I think* cloning a pet might be OK.

5. Lara: *That's amazing!*

6. Lara: *That's strange.*

7. Andy: *It's a bit expensive.*

8. Lara: *I think* it's better to get one that is already alive...

F *(page 150)* Answers will vary.

LESSON TASK: GROUP DEBATES ON CLONING

(page 151)

Review the steps with the class. For multi-level classes, be sure to group lower level students with higher level students.

(page 151)

Ask groups to share their results with the class. Point out the sample sentence and encourage students to use it as a model when they share their results.

(page 151)

Review the steps for doing the debate. Give groups time to prepare their ideas. Have a timer ready to ensure equal time for both groups. For multi-level groups, be sure that everyone has a part, but encourage the higher level students to present the more complex ideas.

ANSWER KEY

LESSON TASK

A–C *(page 151)* Answers will vary.

Video

VIEWING: *A CHANCE TO SEE AGAIN* *(page 152)*

Overview of the Video

The video introduces the work of Dr. Helena Ndume from Namibia. Once a refugee, Dr. Ndume worked hard to become an eye doctor and now helps the blind in her country. She is the first recipient of the United Nations Nelson Mandela Prize.

BEFORE VIEWING

A *(page 152)*

Review the answers by saying the definition aloud and asking volunteers to say the matching word.

B Critical Thinking: Analyzing Visuals *(page 152)*

Be sure students look at the map on page 153 before discussing the questions with their partner. Ask students to share the answers to question 1 and their thoughts about question 2 with the class.

> Ideas for… **EXPANSION**
>
> Have students write down other questions related to the map on page 153. Walk around and check their questions to ensure correct grammar. Then divide the class into small groups. Tell them to ask their question to their groupmates.

WHILE VIEWING

C ▶ 1.14 **Understanding Main Ideas** *(page 153)*

Give students time to read the questions before viewing the video.

D ▶ 1.14 **Understanding Details** *(page 153)*

Give students time to read the sentences and the words in the box before viewing the video again.

AFTER VIEWING

E Personalizing *(page 153)*

Invite a student from each group to share their group's answers and ideas.

> Ideas for… **EXPANSION**
>
> As a class, choose one of the ideas that was discussed in exercise E for "giving back" to the community. If possible, make plans outside of class to meet and do this activity together.

ANSWER KEY

VIDEO

A *(page 152)* **1.** f; **2.** d; **3.** a; **4.** b; **5.** e **6.** c

B *(page 152)*

1. It's worse in Africa, India, and other developing or lower-income countries. It's less serious in wealthier (developed) countries.
2. Possible answer:

   It might be worse because there are not enough doctors; people don't have money for doctors.

   Note: Students may guess that people in these countries have genes for blindness, but this does not seem to be the case. It's more about lack of money and access to healthcare.

C *(page 153)* Possible answers:

1. A place where a doctor helps people with eye problems.
2. At first, some people were afraid.
3. They changed their minds and decided it was OK to go the second year because many people were helped the first year. The doctor fixed their blindness and the people could see again.

D *(page 153)* **1.** hospital; **2.** family; **3.** 82; **4.** hurt; **5.** thousands; **6.** help

E *(page 153)* Possible answers:

People can care for older people by walking with them or taking them meals; they can help tutor children; they can give food or clothing to people who need it, and so on.

Lesson B

VOCABULARY

A 2.36 *(page 154)*

Read the words aloud before playing the audio. Ask students to share the meanings of any words they know.

> Ideas for… **CHECKING COMPREHENSION**
>
> Check students' understanding of the vocabulary words by asking the following questions to the class. Be sure to have them use the vocabulary word in their response.
>
> 1. Who knows how many *bones* we have in our body? *(206)* How many bones do we have when we are born? *(270)* Why do we have fewer *bones* when we are adults? *(Some bones fuse together.)*
> 2. What are some things that you *replace* in your home often? *(batteries, trash bags, etc.)*
> 3. Do you *consider* yourself *healthy*? Why or why not?
> 4. How can you keep your *heart healthy*?
> 5. Do any of your body *parts* hurt today?
> 6. Do you believe in ancient or traditional ways of medical *treatment*? Or, do you think more modern *treatments* are better?

B 2.37 **Meaning from Context** *(pages 154–155)*

After listening, have students read the paragraphs aloud for pronunciation practice.

C *(page 155)*

Ask for volunteers to read the completed sentences aloud.

D **Personalizing** *(page 155)*

> Ideas for… **EXPANSION**
>
> Divide the class into two teams (or four if it is a large class). Teams will debate whether it is a good idea to get a DNA test done to find out your health in the future. One team will be "Pro DNA Tests" and the other team will be "Con DNA Tests". Give teams time to come up with ideas to support their side. Monitor their work. Allow time for the teams to debate each other. Follow these debate rules:
>
> Allow Team 1 two minutes to explain their side and give reasons.
>
> Allow Team 2 one minute to counter Team 1's reasons.
>
> Allow Team 2 two minutes to explain their side and give reasons.
>
> Allow Team 1 one minute to counter Team 2's reasons.

> Ideas for… **EXPANSION**
>
> Write the following question on the board:
>
> Do you want to get a DNA test to see what your health might be in the future? Or to learn about your family background?
>
> Give students time to think about their opinion, and then have them walk around the room and explain their answer to their classmates. Remind them to use the expressions from the *Speaking Skill* and *Everyday Language* boxes on page 150 for expressing opinions and for agreeing and disagreeing with opinions.

ANSWER KEY

VOCABULARY

C *(page 155)* **1.** bone; **2.** consider; **3.** simple; **4.** treatment; **5.** healthy; **6.** parts; **7.** heart; **8.** replace

D *(page 155)* Answers will vary.

LISTENING: A LECTURE ON ENDING BLINDNESS

BEFORE LISTENING

A Predicting *(page 156)*

Have students share and discuss their predictions with a partner.

> **Ideas for... EXPANSION**
>
> Have small groups brainstorm or research how to keep your eyes healthy. Encourage them to use modals (*could, might, may, will*) when discussing ideas they are sure about and those that they are not sure about. Start the groups off with a few ideas; for example:
>
> *To keep your eyes healthy, you could wear sunglasses on sunny days.*
>
> *Not touching your eyes will keep your eyes healthy.*
>
> After the groups brainstorm, ask students to share their ideas with the class.

WHILE LISTENING

B 2.38 ▶ 1.15 **Listening for Main Ideas** *(page 156)*

Give the students time to read the statements and answer choices before listening to the audio.

C 2.39 ▶ 1.16 **Listening for Main Ideas** *(page 157)*

Play the audio a second time to allow students to check their answers. Review answers as a class on the board.

D 2.40 **Listening for Details** *(page 157)*

To review, have students read aloud the completed sentences.

E Checking Predictions *(page 157)*

Ask students which answers they predicted correctly. Ask them to raise their hands for each. For students who did not choose the correct answers, ask them which answer they chose and why.

AFTER LISTENING

F Critical Thinking: Evaluating *(page 157)*

Recreate the chart on the board. After the group discussion, ask a few groups to come to the board and write the ideas they discussed in the chart.

ANSWER KEY

LISTENING

A *(page 156)* Correct predictions (not to be checked until later) are: **1.** b; **2.** a; **3.** b

B *(page 156)* **1.** b; **2.** b; **3.** a

C *(page 157)*

1. unhealthy, healthy

2. eye, grow

3. replace, part

D *(page 157)* **1.** 39; **2.** 10; **3.** 20; **4.** smallest; **5.** your parents; **6.** a machine; **7.** stem; **8.** don't yet

E *(page 157)* Answers will vary.

F *(page 157)* Possible answers:

DNA Research in Medicine	
Pros (a good idea)	Cons (not a good idea)
Treatment could help people and their families; it could change people's lives for the better; it might save lives.	The treatment might fail; it could possibly hurt someone; someone could die as a result; it might be very expensive and difficult to pay back.

SPEAKING

Ideas for… PRESENTING PRONUNCIATION: Schwa /ə/ in Unstressed Syllables

2.41 Write the words in the Pronunciation box on the board: *become, machine, replace*. Ask students to repeat the words and notice the stressed syllables. Then ask them to repeat the words and identify the sound in the underlined syllable (sounds like a fast *uh*). Explain that this is the *schwa* sound and that often unstressed syllables in words sound like schwa (but not always!)

A 2.42 *(page 158)*

Say all the words aloud first, and then have the students mark the unstressed syllables on their own.

B 2.43 *(page 158)*

Walk around and monitor the students reading the text aloud. Provide feedback on their pronunciation and make suggestions on how to put more or less stress on the words.

C *(page 159)*

Ask students to share what they know about DNA research in the jobs listed as well as any other jobs. Ask if any of the jobs sound interesting to them.

Ideas for… EXPANSION

Discuss the fact that many criminals have been released from prison after being proven innocent by DNA testing. Ask the students' opinion on whether we should go back to check the DNA testing of every criminal case.

ANSWER KEY

SPEAKING

A *(page 158)* Schwa syllables are underlined

1. bi-o-lo-gy; **2.** tech-no-lo-gy; **3.** ther-a-py; **4.** pro-blem; **5.** com-pu-ter; **6.** sci-en-tist; **7.** con-trol; **8.** cri-mi-nal

B *(page 158)* **1.** Scientists; **2.** becoming; **3.** can; **4.** information; **5.** police; **6.** computer; **7.** technology; **8.** could

C *(page 159)* Possible answers:

- biologists/earth scientists: As introduced in Unit 6, DNA might be used to look at the impact of plastics on animals, or to identify new species.
- historians/archaeologists: As the Unit 7 video shows, extinct species such as dinosaurs are tested to see relationships to each other and to animals today.
- police: As introduced in this unit, DNA might be used to find criminals.
- lawyers: As introduced in this unit, lawyers may use the information in court to help show that someone is innocent or guilty.
- computer scientists: As introduced in this unit, DNA might be used to write programs to analyze DNA data; maybe help companies that provide personal family research (e.g., Ancestry.com, FamilyTreeDNA, etc.)

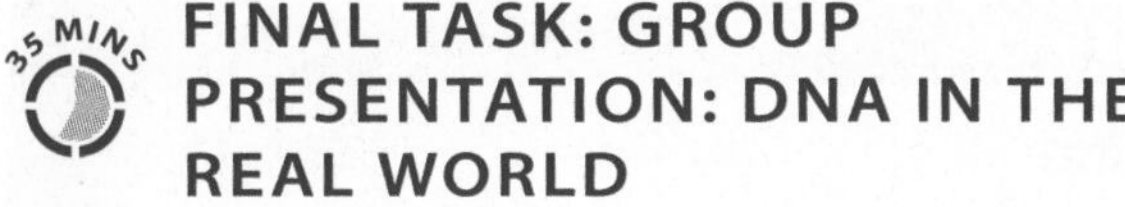

FINAL TASK: GROUP PRESENTATION: DNA IN THE REAL WORLD

A *(page 159)*

Give groups time to look through the unit and research some ideas for their group presentation.

B **Brainstorming** *(page 159)*

Monitor the groups' brainstorming sessions. Help them think of more ideas if necessary and make sure students stay focused on the topic.

C **Organizing Ideas** *(page 160)*

Review the outline and point out the questions that will help with organizing their ideas.

D *(page 160)*

Help the groups with thinking of and writing their questions if necessary. Remind them that they should be able to answer the question themselves or at least offer opinions or ideas about it.

E *(page 160)*

Remind students to practice their presentations before presenting to the class. If the class is large, divide the class into two groups to give their presentations. Remind students how to be a good audience.

ANSWER KEY

FINAL TASK

A–E *(page 159–160)* Answers will vary.

REFLECTION

- Have students answer questions 1–2 on their own.
- Have them discuss their answers in pairs or small groups.
- Ask students to discuss similarities and differences in their answers for questions 1–2. For question 3, have students compare answers and then write the words they are still unsure of on the board. Lead a class review of the challenging words and reteach terms as necessary.

AUDIO SCRIPTS

CD1

Unit 1: Same and Different

LESSON A Vocabulary

Track 1.2 A. Page 4

favorite
friendly
hobby
kind
music
science
shy
vacation

Track 1.3 B. Meaning from Context Page 4

Male Hi, I am Abdul. I'm from Saudi Arabia. I speak Arabic. I also speak English. I like all sports. My favorite sport is soccer. I like to listen to rock music and jazz. My favorite school subject is science. I am very friendly. I like to laugh and have fun.

Female Hi, I am Claudia and I'm from Brazil. I speak Portuguese and English. In my country, volleyball is popular. I play volleyball on my school team. My favorite kind of music is pop. My hobby is reading. I read two books each week! I am shy and like to spend time alone. I love to go to the beach on vacation.

Listening: A Lecture on Twins

Track 1.4 C. Listening for Main Ideas Page 6

Male Student: Identical means *exactly the same*.

Professor: Yes, that's right, but when we talk about identical twins, are they *exactly* the same?

Female Student: I think they look the same, but maybe they don't act the same? Like, one is shy and the other is friendly.

Professor: Yes. That is possibly true. But, first let's look at the science. Do you know how identical twins are formed?

Female Student: I think identical twins are from one egg.

Professor: Yes, so they are more alike than twins that come from two eggs, or *fraternal* twins.

Male Student: So, is that why they look the same?

Professor: Yes. But what do you think? Do they also *act* the same way?

Some scientists study this. They look at identical twins who did not live with each other. They lived with different families and possibly lived in different towns. Some never met each other.

The Jim twins are one of my favorite examples. In 1939, the Jim twins were born in Ohio. When they were four weeks old, they went to different families. Interestingly, both families named their son James, or Jim for short. The two Jims met each other for the first time when they were 39 years old, and were very surprised when they met. Both are six feet tall and weigh 180 pounds. Both were police officers and had wives named Linda. They both even had *second* wives named Betty. Both had dogs named Toy. They both took family vacations in St. Petersburg, Florida. They both named a son James Alan. They were both good at math and bad at spelling. They both like to make things with wood as a hobby, *and* they both drive the same kind of car. They grew up in different homes with different parents but they are the same in many ways.

Male Student: So, are all identical twins the same like this?

Professor: Good question. I was just going to say that it's important to note that not all identical twins are exactly the same. They may come from the same egg, but identical twins can be very different from one another. For example, they may have different hobbies, like to play different sports, or prefer different kinds of music. Also, some twins act very differently. Even in the case of the Jim Twins, there are some differences. As I said, they both named their son James Alan, but Jim Lewis spelled "Alan," A-l-a-n and Jim Springer spelled "Alan," A-l-l-a-n. Some other differences are that James Lewis married three times, but James Springer married two times. Also, James Lewis has long hair, but James Springer has short hair.

fade out

Track 1.5 D. Listening for Details Page 6

Professor: ... The Jim twins are one my favorite examples. In 1939, the Jim twins were born in Ohio. When they were four weeks old, they went to different families. Interestingly, both families named their son James, or Jim for short. The two Jims met each other for the first time when they were 39 years old, and were very surprised when they met. Both are six feet tall and weigh 180 pounds. Both were police officers and had wives named Linda. They both even had *second* wives named Betty. Both had dogs named Toy. They both took family vacations in St. Petersburg, Florida. They both named a son James Alan. They were both good at math and bad at spelling. They both like to make things with wood as a hobby, *and* they both drive the same kind of car. They grew up in different homes with different parents but they are the same in many ways.

Track 1.6 E. Note Taking Page 7

Professor: ...The Jim twins are one my favorite examples. In 1939, the Jim twins were born in Ohio. When they were four weeks old, they went to different families. Interestingly, both families named their son James, or Jim for short. The two Jims met each other for the first time when they were 39 years old, and were very surprised when they met. Both are six feet tall and weigh 180 pounds. Both were police officers and had wives named Linda. They both even had *second* wives named Betty. Both had dogs named Toy. They both took family vacations in St. Petersburg, Florida. They both named a son James Alan. They were both good at math and bad at spelling. They both like to make things with wood as a hobby, *and* they both drive the same kind of car. They grew up in different homes with different parents but they are the same in many ways.

Student: Are all identical twins the same like this?

Professor: Good question, I was just going to say that it's important to note that not all identical twins are exactly the same. They may come from the same egg, but identical twins can be very different from one another. For example, they may have different hobbies, like to play different sports and listen to different kinds of music. Also, some twins act very differently. Even in the case of the Jim Twins, there are some differences. As I said, they both named their son James Alan, but Jim Lewis spelled "Alan," A-l-a-n and Jim Springer spelled "Alan," A-l-l-a-n. Some other differences are that James Lewis married three times, but James Springer married two times. Also, James Lewis has long hair, but James Springer has short hair.

Speaking

Track 1.7 A. Page 8

Meet Chris Bashinelli

There are many National Geographic Explorers. This is Chris Bashinelli. His nickname is "Bash." He was born in New York. His parents were his heroes. They taught him to travel and learn about the world.

In the past, Chris was an actor, but he isn't an actor now. It was fun, but it wasn't the job for him. He wanted to travel and see the world, so he went to Tanzania. Many people in Tanzania are very poor, but they aren't unhappy. Chris learned that you don't need to have a lot of money to have a good life.

The trip changed his life. Now he is a storyteller. He has a show on TV (National Geographic Channel). Chris's show is *Bridge the Gap*. It is on TV in over 100 countries around the world!

Track 1.8 C. Page 9

A: Hi, I'm Muhammad. This is my friend Samir. What's your name?

B: My name is Miguel. Are you two from here?

C: No. We're not Americans. We're from the United Arab Emirates. Where are you from?

B: I'm from California. pause, then inquiringly ask Are you guys students?

A: We were students last year, but now we're teachers. Are you a student?

B: No. chuckle I was a student many years ago, but, now I'm a teacher, too.

C: Well, it was nice to meet you, Miguel. fade

Track 1.9 E. Page 10

Conversation 1: In class

A: I am from China. Where are you from?

B: I'm from Australia. What do you do?

A: I'm a student. How about you?

B: I'm a writer.

A: It's nice to meet you.

B: Nice to meet you, too.

Conversation 2: In an elevator

A: Can you believe this weather? It's so cold.

B: Tell me about it! Yesterday was so nice!

Conversation 3: At a party

A: Hi. I'm Yoko. And, you're Nadia, right?

B: Yes.

A: Do you play any sports?

B: Yes. I play tennis and I also do judo.

A: That's great. I don't play sports, but I have a lot of hobbies.

B: What are your hobbies?

A: I read books and play chess.

LESSON B Vocabulary

Track 1.10 A. Page 14

adult
change
grow up
parents
teenager
typical
the world
years old

Track 1.11 B. Meaning from Context Page 14

QUIZ: How Typical are you?

The world now has seven billion people. What is a typical person? Are you typical? Or are you different? *Typical* means different things in every country. Take the quiz. Your opinion of what *typical* means may change.

To check your answers, keep listening. To take the quiz, press stop. pause

1. A typical size man in Holland is 5 feet, 11 inches tall, but a typical size man in Peru is 5 feet, 4 inches.
2. A typical Japanese woman lives to be 86 years old, but a typical woman from Afghanistan lives to be 45 years old.
3. A child becomes an adult in Saudi Arabia and Indonesia at 15 years old, but in the United Arab Emirates and Singapore, the age is 21.
4. In the United States, 69% of children grow up in families with both parents, but 87% of children from India grow up in families with both parents.
5. A typical teenager (13–19 years old) in the United States sends 30 text messages a day, but a typical Japanese teenager sends 100 text messages every day.
6. In Italy, 80% of young adults live at home with their parents before they get married, but in Canada, only 30% of young adults live with their parents before marriage.

Listening: A Conversation about the Teenage Brain

Track 1.12 C. Listening for Main Ideas and D. Listening for Main Ideas Page 17

Professor Diaz: Come in!

Pedro: Hi, Professor Diaz. Can I ask you a few questions?

Professor Diaz: Oh hi, Pedro. Sure.

Pedro: I know you study teenagers and I'm writing a paper on them. Can you tell me a little bit about the teenage brain?

Professor Diaz: Well, a teenager's brain is still growing.

Pedro: Really?

Professor Diaz: Yes, people stop growing physically around 15 or 16 years old, but our brains continue to grow until we're around twenty-three years old.

Pedro: I didn't know that. So, do all teenagers around the world act the same for this reason?

Professor Diaz: Well, typical teenagers have many feelings. One minute they are sad and the next minute they are happy. Their feelings change very quickly and they think and react to problems and situations very differently from adults.

Pedro: Why does this happen?

Professor Diaz: Scientists found that teenagers use the amygdala part of the brain more than adults do. The amygdala is important for feelings. But after the brain stops growing, adults use another part of the brain, the frontal cortex, more.

Pedro: So, when people use their frontal cortex more, their feelings don't change much?

Professor Diaz: Yes, exactly.

Pedro: Interesting. So, teenagers are all the same because their brain is still growing.

Professor Diaz: Not exactly. Teenagers all go through the same thing as they grow, but teenagers can also be very different from each other.

Pedro: How?

Professor Diaz: Well, in my opinion, there are four main things that make one teenager different from another teenager.

Pedro: What are those?

Professor Diaz: Family, friends, experiences—or the things that happen to them—, and things like TV, magazines, the Internet, and other kinds of *media*. These four things can impact or change a teenager's life greatly.

Pedro: That makes sense. I had a good friend when I was a child. We did everything together, but now she is very different from me. She started doing things with other kids and they got into some bad things.

Professor Diaz: Yes. Many things can change a teenager. This means it's important to watch teenagers closely to make sure their friends are good people and that they have good experiences.

Pedro: Teenagers have a difficult time with all of these changes. What can adults do to help them during these years?

Professor Diaz: Tell them that their feelings are typical for a teenager. It is how we grow up. Tell them to write their feelings in a diary or a journal. This may help them understand their feelings more. Also, tell them to talk with their parents and their family, the people that love them.

Pedro: Well, thank you so much, Professor Diaz. This is very helpful.

Professor Diaz: It's my pleasure. Any time.

Track 1.13 E. Listening for Details — Page 17

Professor Diaz: Well, in my opinion, there are four main things that make one teenager different from another teenager.

Pedro: What are those?

Professor Diaz: Family, friends, experiences—or the things that happen to them—, and things like TV, magazines, the Internet, and other kinds of *media*. These four things can impact or change a teenager's life greatly.

Speaking

Track 1.14 Pronunciation: Contractions with *Be* — Page 18

I'm a teenager.	*I'm not an adult.*
You're 16 years old?	*You aren't 15? You're not 15?*
It's typical K-pop music.	*It isn't the kind of music I like.*
She wasn't a typical teenager.	*They weren't typical teenagers.*

Track 1.15 A. — Page 18

1. I'm not shy.
2. It is typical to feel that way.
3. He isn't a teenager. He's an adult.
4. She is a child. She is six years old.
5. We're not only brothers. We're twins.
6. They aren't my parents. They're my friends.

Unit 2: Love Your Job

LESSON A Vocabulary

Track 1.16 A. — Page 24

boring
boss
create
exciting
satisfied
together
try
work

Track 1.17 B. Meaning from Context — Page 24

How U.S. Workers Feel About Their Jobs

Before we talk about the kinds of jobs that are available today, let's look at some statistics, or numbers. It seems that more and more people are satisfied with their work.

- If we look at the chart, we see that 88 percent of US workers are satisfied with their job. It is good to see that people are happy in their work.
- As far as what is important in a job, we see that 53 percent of workers think a good boss is important. I agree with this.
- Moving on, we see that 48 percent of workers think their work is exciting. Hmmm. Well, we can't all have exciting jobs!
- The chart also shows that 43 percent of workers think that working together with other people is important.
- A surprising number of people create their own jobs. The chart shows that 14 percent of workers create their own job. That's amazing!
- This number makes bosses happy: 86 percent of workers try hard at their job.
- And this number is a good sign also: only 2 percent of people think their job is boring.

So, all in all—these numbers look really good for our job market. Fade on this last line

Listening: Online Lecture: Who's happy at work?

Track 1.18 B. Listening for Main Ideas and C. — Page 26

Are you satisfied with your work? Today we are talking about job satisfaction, or the things people need to be happy at work. What do you think is most important to people? You might be surprised that it is *not* money!

One thing that many people look for: a job that helps other people. In general, people want to help other people; they want to make the world a better place. Teachers are normally at the top of the list of happiest jobs. Every day, teachers help people learn and grow. Think about your favorite teacher. Most likely, he or she was happy at work.

Another thing people want from a job is to create things. They want to use their minds; they don't want to be in a boring job. They don't want to sit at a desk every day and look at a computer. Engineers are also usually at the top of the list of happiest jobs. Engineers create new products. It's very exciting when they finally see their new product. When was the last time you made something? Did it make you happy?

Also, people want their boss to thank them for the work they do. When a boss thanks their workers for their good work, they feel more satisfied with their jobs. And when people are satisfied in their jobs, they try hard.

Finally, people want to have happy co-workers. Everybody wants to enjoy their day at work. When co-workers work hard, like their job, and are friendly, there's a good work environment. A job is a lot of fun when you work together with other happy people.

Of course, there are other things that people look for in a job. Money matters, and where you work is important, but overall, being happy is most important to many people.

Track 1.19 D. Page 27

One thing that many people look for: a job that helps other people. In general, people want to help other people; they want to make the world a better place. Teachers are normally at the top of the list of happiest jobs. Every day, teachers help people learn and grow. Think about your favorite teacher. Most likely, he or she was happy at work.

Another thing people want from a job is to create things. They want to use their minds; they don't want to be in a boring job. They don't want to sit at a desk every day and look at a computer. Engineers are also usually at the top of the list of happiest jobs. Engineers create new products. It's very exciting when they finally see their new product. When was the last time you made something? Did it make you happy?

Also, people want their boss to thank them for the work they do. When a boss thanks their workers for their good work, they feel more satisfied with their jobs. And when people are satisfied in their jobs, they try hard.

Finally, people want to have happy co-workers. Everybody wants to enjoy their day at work. When co-workers work hard, like their job, and are friendly, there's a good work environment. A job is a lot of fun when you work together with other happy people.

Track 1.20 E. Listening for Details Page 27

One thing that many people look for: a job that helps other people. In general, people want to help other people; they want to make the world a better place. Teachers are normally at the top of the list of happiest jobs. Every day, teachers help people learn and grow. Think about your favorite teacher. Most likely, he or she was happy at work.

Another thing people want from a job is to create things. They want to use their minds; they don't want to be in a boring job. They don't want to sit at a desk every day and look at a computer. Engineers are also usually at the top of the list of happiest jobs. Engineers create new products. It's very exciting when they finally see their new product. When was the last time you made something? Did it make you happy?

Speaking

Track 1.21 Pronunciation: Simple Present -*s* Form of the Verb Page 29

The -*s*/-*es* sounds like:

- /s/ after verbs ending in: /f/, /k/, /p/, /t/
  laughs, works, keeps, meets
- /z/ after verbs ending in: /b/, /d/, /g/, /l/, /m/, /n/, /ng/, /r/, /v/ and all vowel sounds.
  needs, calls, begins, moves, sees, goes
- /əz after verbs ending in: /s/, /sh/, /ch/, /z/, /j/
  misses, mixes, pushes, teaches, uses, judges

Track 1.22 E. Page 29

1. creates
2. reads
3. fixes
4. gives
5. knows
6. washes
7. helps
8. tries
9. catches
10. sits

Track 1.23 F. Page 29

There are many things I do for my job. First, I talk to customers all day. I help them find what they need. I read and learn all about the products because I explain how to use the products we sell in the store and show them to customers. There are times when I don't know the answer to a question and so I call the company to get the answer for the customer. I don't use a computer often for my work and that's OK with me. I don't like computers. I like to be with people.

LESSON B Vocabulary

Track 1.24 A. Page 34

advice
company
contacts
enjoy
fail
manager
own
skills

Track 1.25 B. Meaning from Context Page 34

Career Advice from an Artist

I always say: *Life is short, so love what you do.* You should *always* enjoy your work. Here's some great advice someone gave me when I was young:

First, think about what you are good at and use the skills you already have. Are you good with people? Are you creative? Do you want to be a manager or a supervisor? Or do *you* want to be the boss and maybe have your own business some day? I started my company when I was just 25. It was scary, but also exciting!

Second, when you begin to look for a job, start with your family and friends. These contacts can help you find a job. As they say, it's not *what* you know, but *who* you know.

Finally, remember that you may fail at first, but don't quit. Keep trying, again and again, to do what you love!

Listening: An Interview about 21st Century Jobs

Track 1.26 B. Listening for Main Ideas Page 36

Presenter: If you're having trouble finding a job that is right for you, then maybe you need to create your own job. Today, we will be talking with Natalia Stewart, a career advisor, who helps people find the right job. Welcome, Natalia!

Natalia Stewart: Thank you.

P: So, tell us. Are many people creating their own jobs nowadays?

NS: Yes, they are. People create new jobs each year. These are jobs we didn't have 5 or 10 years ago.

P: How do people create new jobs?

NS: Well, in a few different ways. One, we live in the computer age and things are changing every year. And two, people are creative. People need things and other people see this need and they do something about it.

P: What are some examples of new technology jobs?

NS: Well, now that every company is online and apps for smartphones make so much money, there are lots of new jobs related to technology. For example, app designers, app developers, and cloud specialists.

P: Ahh. Yes, the digital age is really creating a lot of new jobs, but what is a cloud Specialist? I have never heard of that before.

NS: Well, the cloud is where we keep things on the Internet. Like some people keep all of their photos in the cloud. So, a cloud specialist is a person who manages this technology.

P: Interesting. Any other new jobs?

NS: Yes. As you know, companies show and sell their product through social media sites. So, new jobs such as bloggers and social media managers are very popular today.

P: Bloggers and social media managers! These jobs probably sound like a different language to our grandparents! Besides these technology jobs, what other new jobs are there?

NS: Well, there are many kinds of new jobs such as sleep coaches—they teach babies and their parents how to sleep; life coaches—they help people be satisfied with their lives; and playlist professionals.

P: What's a playlist professional?

NS: They create playlists—or lists of songs—for companies to use in their stores, on their TV or radio commercials, or on their websites.

P: So, they just choose the songs?

NS: Yes—they find out about the company and the kind of customer they want and they create a song list to use.

P: What a fun job!

NS: Yes, especially if you enjoy music. And, that's what creating your own job is all about---doing something that you love with the skills that you have—such as talking to people, or being good with numbers or technology. It takes a lot of time to create a new job, so it's better to do something you enjoy.

P: I see. So, a hobby or your favorite sport or something?

NS: Yes. Think of a way to make your hobby into a job.

P: Any other advice?

NS: Yes, four things, in fact. First, as I already said, do what you enjoy and use the skills that you have. Second, ask the question: what do people need? Third, talk to all of your contacts—your friends, your friends' friends, your parents' friends. Contacts are important in business. And, fourth, just try it. Don't listen to people who tell you that you're crazy. Just try. Yes, maybe you'll fail, but you can keep trying until you get it right.

P: I agree. When you fail, it helps you get better. Great advice, Natalia. Thank you.

Track 1.27 C. Page 36

P: So, tell us. Are many people creating their own jobs nowadays?

NS: Yes, they are. People create new jobs each year. These are jobs we didn't have 5 or 10 years ago.

P: How do people create new jobs?

NS: Well, in a few different ways. One, we live in the computer age and things are changing every year. And two, people are creative. People need things and other people see this need and they do something about it.

Track 1.28 D. Note Taking Page 37

P: Any other advice?

NS: Yes, four things, in fact. First, as I already said, do what you enjoy and use the skills that you have. Second, ask the question: what do people need? Third, talk to all of your contacts—your friends, your friends' friends, your parents' friends. Contacts are important in business. And, fourth, just try it. Don't listen to people who tell you that you're crazy. Just try. Yes, maybe you'll fail, but you can keep trying until you get it right.

Track 1.29 E. Listening for Details Page 37

NS: Well, now that every company is online and apps for smartphones make so much money, there are lots of new jobs related to technology. For example, app designers, app developers, and cloud specialists.

P: Ahh. Yes, the digital age is really creating a lot of new jobs, but what is a cloud specialist? I have never heard of that before.

NS: Well, the cloud is where we keep things on the Internet. Like some people keep all of their photos in the cloud. So, a cloud specialist is a person who manages this technology.

P: Interesting. Any other new jobs?

NS: Yes. As you know, companies show and sell their product through social media sites. So, new jobs such as bloggers and social media managers are very popular today.

P: Bloggers and social media managers! These jobs probably sound like a different language to our grandparents! Besides these technology jobs, what other new jobs are there?

NS: Well, there are many kinds of new jobs such as sleep coaches—they teach babies and their parents how to sleep; life coaches—they help people be satisfied with their lives; and playlist professionals.

P: What's a playlist professional?

NS: They create playlists—or lists of songs—for companies to use in their stores, on their TV or radio commercials, or on their websites.

P: So, they just choose the songs?

NS: Yes—they find out about the company and the kind of customer they want and they create a song list to use.

P: What a fun job!

NS: Yes, especially if you enjoy music.

Unit 3: Unusual Destinations

LESSON A Vocabulary

Track 1.30 A. Page 44

area
beautiful
crowded
famous
quiet
tourists
unusual
visit

Track 1.31 B. Meaning from Context Page 44

Fatima: Hi Arturo. I'm trying to plan my summer vacation. Should I go to the beach, like I always do? Or should I try a famous place, like Paris? Or maybe a new and very different destination-- somewhere unusual? What do you think?

Arturo: I think you should try somewhere unusual! I saw a TV show about an amazing glacier in Greenland. It's called Eqi Glacier. The ice on the glacier is so clear and the snow is very white. It's so beautiful. Not many people go there, so it's not crowded.

Fatima: Hmm. It sounds like a great place to visit, especially in the hot summer months! And I like that there aren't many tourists there. I like to go to quiet places. In my opinion, the fewer people, the better!

Arturo: Well, it looks like a great area where you can relax and have fun!

Listening: Presentation: Unusual Southeast Asia

Track 1.32 C. Listening for Main Ideas Page 47

Presenter (Tom): Welcome to the Fifth Annual Travel Convention: Unusual Destinations. Our first speaker is Susana Jenkins. She travels around the world and writes blogs and books about her adventures. She recently returned from a trip to Southeast Asia, and she's here today to share her ideas about a few interesting and unusual places to visit. Please help me welcome Susana Jenkins. applause

Susana Jenkins: Thank you. Thank you, it's nice to be here today. As Tom just told you, I recently visited Southeast Asia for a new book I'm writing, and today, I'll tell you about three of the countries I went to.

Many tourists visit Southeast Asia, and usually they go to the well-travelled places: the beaches and islands of southern Thailand, big cities such as Singapore or Bangkok with their beautiful temples and palaces, or the very famous sites such as Angkor Wat in Cambodia or the island of Bali in Indonesia. These places are certainly great to visit, yet they can be very crowded. So, I like to go to the more *unusual* places—beautiful areas that few tourists know about.

First, I'd like to show you some photos from my trip. I started my trip in Central Java, in Indonesia. Here I am in a rice field. The view is wonderful. As you can see in the picture, these rice paddies are in the mountains. They look like steps in the mountain. They are like a work of art. They are such a quiet, peaceful, and beautiful part of the country, and not many tourists ever see them.

After Indonesia, I went to Thailand. As I said, there are many tourists on Thailand's beaches, so I like to go to a quiet inland part of the country, away from the beaches. One of my favorite places to visit is the wetland area of Northeast Thailand. Here is lovely Red Lotus Lake. You can go out on a boat from December through March and see thousands of lotus flowers in the water. It is breathtaking to see.

Finally, my last destination was in Vietnam. The markets in the town of Sapa are lively and colorful. You can shop or just enjoy looking around. The nearby mountains are tall, green, and beautiful. You can hike along the mountain top and look down into the valley. You feel like you are in the clouds.

So next time you are planning a trip to Southeast Asia—or anywhere—please think about visiting a more unusual destination.

Track 1.33 D. and E. Listening for Details Page 47

First, I'd like to show you some photos from my trip. I started my trip in Central Java, in Indonesia. Here I am in a rice field. The view is wonderful. As you can see in the picture, these rice paddies are in the mountains. They look like steps in the mountain. They are like a work of art. They are such a quiet, peaceful, and beautiful part of the country, and not many tourists ever see them.

After Indonesia, I went to Thailand. As I said, there are many tourists on Thailand's beaches, so I like to go to a quiet inland part of the country, away from the beaches. One of my favorite places to visit is the wetland area of Northeast Thailand. Here is lovely Red Lotus Lake. You can go out on a boat from December through March and see thousands of lotus flowers in the water. It is breathtaking to see.

Finally, my last destination was in Vietnam. The markets in the town of Sapa are lively and colorful. You can shop or just enjoy looking around. The nearby mountains are tall, green, and beautiful. You can hike along the mountain top and look down into the valley. You feel like you are in the clouds.

So next time you are planning a trip to Southeast Asia—or anywhere—please think about visiting a more unusual destination.

Speaking

Track 1.34 A. Page 48

1. **A:** I like exciting vacations.
   B: That's interesting. I don't. I like quiet vacations.
2. **A:** I don't like to go to crowded areas.
   B: I don't, either.
3. **A:** I like to go on adventures!
   B: Me, too!
4. **A:** I don't like to visit the beach.
   B: Oh, really? I do!
5. **A:** I like to visit famous places.
   B: I do, too.

Track 1.35 C. Page 49

A: Hi. What are you doing?

B: I'm looking at my photos from Egypt.

A: What are you doing in this photo?

B: Oh, I'm riding on a camel. In this photo, my friends and I are walking on the beach.

A: It's beautiful! What about this photo?

B: My friend is driving a motorcycle through Cairo.

A: Wow! Sounds exciting!

B: Yes, at times. Oh, in this photo, my friends and I are walking up the pyramids. And, here is a photo of all of us. We are resting halfway up.

A: Funny! Well, at least you're smiling.

LESSON B Vocabulary

Track 1.36 A. Page 54

amazing
island
manmade
mix
modern
natural
special
view

Track 1.37 B. Meaning from Context Page 54

A Manmade Wonder

There are many beautiful places on Earth. Some are natural, like beaches or mountains and others are manmade like tall buildings or parks. One unusual destination in Dubai has a good mix of both. It is a manmade island close to the coast and it looks like a palm tree. The view of the island from an airplane is amazing! The hotel is very new and modern with everything you need or want while on vacation. This destination provides a good mix of nature, beauty, excitement, and relaxation. It is a very special and unusual vacation place.

Listening: A Conversation about a Vacation

Track 1.38 B. Listening for Main Ideas and C. Note Taking Pages 56–57

Juan: Hey, Maria! How was your vacation?

Maria: It was so amazing!

Juan: Where did you go?

Maria: Well, you know me - I'm always looking for unusual places to visit. This year it was definitely unusual! The ICEHOTEL is a hotel made from ice and snow. It's in Lapland, Sweden; about 200 km north of the Arctic Circle. In November, when there is no sun, builders and ice artists from around the world come together to create the hotel. They put snow onto steel walls and after the snow freezes, they take the steel walls away and the snow walls stay up. Each year, the ICEHOTEL looks different. Some years it's very modern. Can you believe they create a new hotel each winter? This year was ICEHOTEL number 26 and there were 57 rooms. The hotel is open from December to April. In the spring, the sun comes out and the snow melts. Then, they start to think about next year's hotel.

Juan: What's it like inside?

Maria: Well, it's very cold, but it's comfortable. The temperature stays between minus 5 and minus 8 degrees Celsius. You dress in warm clothes and a hat and it's not that bad.

Juan: How do you sleep?

Maria: At night, you sleep in a warm sleeping bag on a special bed of ice and animal skins.

Juan: So, even the *beds* are made of ice?

Maria: Yes. All the furniture is made of ice and there is amazing ice art all around the hotel.

Juan: Wow, that sounds so cold! Can you take a bath or shower?

Maria: Well, actually, there is a warm area of the hotel. The bathrooms are in that area. In the morning, they give you hot fruit juice in your bed and then you go to the sauna before breakfast in the main restaurant. I recommend that you only sleep one night in the ICEHOTEL and then go to a regular hotel. There's one nearby.

Juan: Was there a view out of your window?

Maria: The view from our bedroom window was nice. Lots of snow!

Juan: How beautiful and quiet.

Maria: Yes, it was beautiful--but not so quiet. There were a lot of people at the hotel that night. It was crowded!

Juan: Where were they from?

Maria: I was surprised at the mix of people there. Not many local people, though-- mostly tourists from Europe and the United States.

Juan: Wow! What an adventure!

Maria: Yes, it was an amazing place to visit. It was both natural and manmade; a good mix!

Juan: Do you have photos?

Maria: Oh, yes. In this one, I am sitting at the table in the restaurant. In this one, my sister is relaxing on the bed. And in this photo, my sister is looking at the ice art.

Juan: Great pictures. Thanks for sharing! Will you go again next year?

Maria: I like to do different things each year so next vacation, I want to go somewhere warm.

Juan: I heard there are some beautiful manmade islands in Dubai.

Maria: That's an interesting idea!

Speaking

Track 1.39 Pronunciation: Syllables and Stress Page 58

One-syllable words: rice rice, book book

Two-syllable words: island is-land, advice ad-vice

Three-syllable words: beautiful beau-ti-ful, amazing a-ma-zing

Track 1.40 A. Page 58

1. hotel
2. love
3. vacation
4. special
5. area
6. together
7. view
8. company
9. manager
10. famous

Unit 4: High Tech, No Tech

LESSON A Vocabulary

Track 1.41 A. Page 64

benefit
download
equipment
experience
hard
the past
prepare
real

Track 1.42 B. Meaning from Context Page 64

America's National Parks Go Virtual

Today, you can go on a journey through the national parks and experience the beauty without ever leaving your home. Some national parks in the United States have a virtual reality (VR) tour. You do not need to prepare for a long trip any more. It's not hard at all; it's very easy. You can just download the National Park VR app, put on some VR glasses and, in no time, you feel like you are in Yosemite National Park. It is always better to see the real thing, but a VR tour allows anyone to see the park at any time! It can cost a lot of money to visit the parks so the VR tour gives you the opportunity to experience the beautiful views without spending a lot. In the past, the only ways to see the parks were to travel there, look at photos, or watch a video. Another benefit of visiting the park virtually is that it will not be crowded. Any time you are ready, just put on your VR equipment and go!

Listening: A Conversation about Virtual Reality

Track 1.43 B. Listening for Main Ideas and D. Listening for Details Pages 66–67

Lily: Hi, Paul. What are you doing?

Paul: Oh, hi, Lily. I'm preparing for a presentation I'm giving about virtual reality.

Lily: Virtual reality? I thought that was just for video gaming! Where you put goggles or glasses on and it feels like you're doing the things that you're seeing?

Paul: Exactly. It's so cool. I found this one company that creates lessons and materials for schools using virtual reality.

Lily: What happened to the old way of teaching? Like in the past? A book and a teacher?

Paul: I know, I know. Many people aren't ready for this new technology, but it's amazing and I know it will help students learn so much more.

Lily: How? What are the benefits? How can it help students learn?

Paul: Well, research shows that students learn best when they do or experience something. If students are learning about a time in history, let's say the sinking of the Titanic or the first trip to the moon, then it's best to learn it by seeing it for real with their own eyes.

Lily: But, it's not *real*!

Paul: I know! There is no way it can be real since it happened in the past. But, it's better than just reading about it. Books can't give them the whole experience.

Lily: Well, what about school trips? Don't you think that it's better for students to go to the real places and be able to see, touch, and feel the real things? Like last year, when I went to Paris and I touched the Eiffel Tower—that was amazing!

Paul: Yes. Of course, it's best to see and experience the real thing, but not all families can pay to send their children to France!

Lily: I guess. Tell me more.

Paul: Well, the virtual reality device takes you to wherever or whenever you want to go. Students can see the deserts of the Middle East, or the Himalayan Mountains up close. They can walk through the great plains of Africa, or swim with the blue whales. The students can even go inside a human body to learn about how our bodies work. If the class is learning about art, they can go to an art museum and take a virtual tour. Or, if they are learning about history, then the class can learn about how the Egyptians built the Great Pyramids or why the Chinese built the Great Wall.

Lily: That's very cool! So, how does it work? Is it hard to do?

Paul: No, it's very easy, in fact. First, you need the equipment. The basics are: a headset, a controller, and a smartphone.

Lily: That's it? That's not hard at all!

Paul: No—it's not. It's easy to buy headsets nowadays, or you can even make your own out of cardboard!

Lily: Then what do you do?

Paul: First, download an app on your phone. There are many Virtual Reality Educational Apps you can get for free. Second, put your phone in the headset. Third, put the headset on so it fits well on your head. Finally, use your controller to open the app and begin. And away you go!

Lily: Well, this is all amazing. Good luck with the presentation! I hope it goes well!

Track 1.44 C. Page 67

Lily: Then what do you do?

Paul: First, download an app on your phone. There are many Virtual Reality Educational Apps you can get for free. Second, put your phone in the headset. Third, put the headset on so it fits well on your head. Finally, use your controller to open the app and begin. And away you go!

Lily: Well, this is all amazing. Good luck with the presentation! I hope it goes well!

Speaking

Track 1.45 Pronunciation: *Can* and *Can't* Page 68

Kuri can talk to people and move around the house.

Kuri can't pick things up or clean your house.

LESSON B Vocabulary

Track 1.46 A. Page 74

available
brain
depend on
effect
health
hurt
rest
worry

Track 1.47 B. Meaning from Context Page 74

Technology News Now

Beware! Your cell phone can be bad for your health! Nowadays, we depend on our cell phones for everything. We use them to check email, send texts, do work, watch movies, listen to music, play games, and even pay our bills. We are always online. We are available for our bosses, our friends, and our families 24 hours a day, 7 days a week. Doctors now say that all of this technology can hurt us.

If you want to do something about this, give your brain a break! Go outside. Go to the park. Take a walk. The fresh air, the beautiful sky, and the trees help give you the rest you need. So, for your next lunch break, go and enjoy the effect of the sunshine. And leave your cell phone at your desk. Don't worry—the world can wait!

Listening: Class Discussion: Taking a Tech Break

Track 1.48 B. Listening for Main Ideas and C. Listening for Details Page 76

Teacher: Good morning everyone. Today's lesson is about the effects your smartphone has on your body, brain, and relationships with other people.

Most people, especially young adults, have a phone with them all the time. We depend on them. We use our phones to text, instant message, and email. We use our phone to shop and download videos, music, and games. We use it to check social media. And there is an app for just about everything nowadays. Some people are on their phones five hours a day!

There is a study that shows that using your phone this much can be bad for your health.

If you're going to take notes, now is a good time to get your pencil and paper ready. A spider map might be helpful for taking notes on this information.

OK, the study goes into detail about the bad effects of using a smartphone. We'll discuss two of the bad effects today: One—smartphones can be bad for your brain. Two—they can be bad for your body.

How do phones have a bad effect on our brain? Well, the first bad effect is attention problems. How many times does your phone beep or ring in one hour? Five? Ten? Twenty times an hour? When you are studying for a big test and your phone is beeping five, ten, twenty times in one hour, do you think you are studying very well? I don't think so. Every time you look at your phone, your attention moves, and this isn't good for your brain.

Another bad effect cell phones have on your brain is in the area of memory. We don't *have* to remember anything anymore because we have all the information we need on our phones.

Mike: That's true. But isn't that a good thing?

Teacher: No, it's important for your brain to remember things. We depend on our smartphones to remember everything—from phone numbers and dates to important facts.

A third reason phones are bad for our brains is the light. The light from your phone wakes up your brain. Your body is tired, but the light tells your brain to stay awake. Your brain needs a rest.

Any questions? The second area I'll talk about is the effects smartphones have on our body. As I talked about, the light from your phone wakes up your brain, but *then* what happens?

Elizabeth: You can't sleep.

Teacher: Right. Our bodies need sleep. Not getting sleep can hurt our bodies. Another reason is that with a smartphone, we are available 24/7, 365.

Mike: What do you mean by 24/7, 365?

Teacher: Someone can talk to you, find you, or ask you a question 24 hours a day, 7 days a week, 365 days a year. To be available all the time creates stress. Stress is bad for our bodies.

Also, with a smartphone, you can see what your friends and the rest of the world are doing 24/7, 365. You can see a picture of some friends on Instagram and you worry that they are having fun without you. This stress and worry is bad for your body. We need to unplug and turn off our phones!

Track 1.49 D. Note Taking Page 77

Teacher: OK, the study goes into detail about the bad effects of using a smartphone. We'll discuss two of the bad effects today: One—smartphones can be bad for your brain. Two—they can be bad for your body.

How do phones have a bad effect on our brain? Well, the first bad effect is attention problems. How many times does your phone beep, or ring in one hour? Five? Ten? Twenty times an hour? When you are studying for a big test and your phone is beeping five, ten, twenty times in one hour, do you think you are studying very well? I don't think so. Every time you look at your phone, your attention moves and this isn't good for your brain.

Another bad effect cell phones have on your brain is in the area of memory. We don't have to remember anything anymore because we have all the information we need on our phones.

Mike: That's true. But isn't that a good thing?

Teacher: No, it's important for your brain to remember things. We depend on our smartphones to remember everything—from phone numbers and dates to important facts.

A third reason phones are bad for our brains is the light. The light from your phone wakes up your brain. Your body is tired, but the light tells your brain to stay awake. Your brain needs a rest.

Any questions? The second area I'll talk about is the effects smartphones have on our body. As I talked about, the light from your phone wakes up your brain, but then what happens?

Elizabeth: You can't sleep.

Teacher: Right. Our bodies need sleep. Not getting sleep can hurt our bodies. Another reason is that with a smartphone, we are available 24/7, 365.

Mike: What do you mean by 24/7, 365?

Teacher: Someone can talk to you, find you, or ask you a question 24 hours a day, 7 days a week, 365 days a year. To be available all the time creates stress. Stress is bad for our bodies.

Also, with a smartphone, you can see what your friends and the rest of the world are doing 24/7, 365. You can see a picture of some friends on Instagram and you worry that they are having fun without you. This stress and worry is bad for your body.

Track 1.50 A. Page 78

A: Are you using any new apps on your phone?

B: Yes, I really like my new walking app. I use it at the gym.

A: How cool! Tell me about it.

B: It's called Virtual Walk. First, you download the app on your phone. Then, you choose a place where you want to walk. You can choose a national park to walk through. You can walk to all of the monuments in Washington DC. There are lots of places to choose.

A: That's so interesting!

B: Next, you get on your treadmill, put on your virtual reality headset, and turn on your app. Then you walk. The virtual reality makes you feel like you are walking in the real place.

A: Really? It feels real?

B: Yes. It's a lot of fun. But, you have to be careful. You can't see the real world with your virtual reality headset on, so sometimes you can fall down.

A: Are you serious? Did that happen to you?

B: Yes, and I hurt my arm.

A: I'm sorry to hear that.

CD2

Unit 5: Risk and Reward

LESSON A Vocabulary

Track 2.2 A. **Page 84**

adventure
body
climb
die
difficult
mind
solve
vote

Track 2.3 B. Meaning from Context **Page 84**

Conversation 1

A: I'm planning to climb K2 next year.

B: Wow! That sounds like a real adventure!

A: Yes, but it's going to be difficult. I have to train every day to get ready.

B: Well, be careful. You can die in the mountains if you're not in shape.

Conversation 2

A: It's important to do different exercises so your whole body becomes stronger, not just your arms, but also your legs, back, and so on.

B: Many people say you should exercise to help your mind, too.

A: Yes. Absolutely. Exercise helps me think a lot more clearly.

Conversation 3

A: Did you vote for the new class president?

B: Yes, I did. Let's hope the winner can solve some of the problems we're having at school.

Listening: Podcast: Adventurer of the Year

Track 2.4 B. Listening for Main Ideas and D. Listening for Details **Pages 86–87**

Michael: Welcome. If you're interested in adventure, you're listening to the right show. This is Adventurer Podcast #201. I'm Michael Day, your host. As usual this time of year, I'd like to tell you about National Geographic's *Adventurer of the Year* award. With me today is student reporter Gina Inaka to tell us about this award. Welcome, Gina.

Gina: Thank you, Michael. I'm happy to be here.

Michael: So, first, can you tell everyone what the *Adventurer of the Year* award is?

Gina: Of course! Each year, National Geographic chooses ten of the best adventurers from around the world. Then people vote for one of these adventurers, and the winner receives the award.

Michael: So, what kind of people does National Geographic choose?

Gina: That's a good question. *Adventurer* can mean different things. An adventurer is often someone who does a dangerous or *extreme* sport like mountain climbing, surfing, or highlining. But someone can be adventurous in their work, too. For example, photographers take pictures of interesting people and places, and explorers travel all over the world and discover many things. They are adventurers, too. Adventurers need a strong body, of course, because their work is not easy. But they also need to solve problems and think quickly, so a good mind is important, too.

Michael: Absolutely! Great points. So, who votes?

Gina: We do! You, or anyone, can go to the website and vote for the person you think is best. The one with the most votes wins the award.

Michael: I see. Can you give us an example? Tell us about one of the winners.

Gina: Sure! The Adventurer of the Year in 2016, for example, was Pasang Lhamu Sherpa Akita. She's a mountain climber from Nepal. She was one of the first Nepali women to climb K2—the second highest mountain in the world and a very difficult one to climb. Also, she was the first female to become a mountain guide in Nepal.

And after Nepal was hit with an earthquake in 2015, she helped bring food, medicine, and other supplies to people. Over 8000 people died in the earthquake. The earthquake hurt millions of people and many lost their homes. She made a big difference there.

Michael: Wow. So, she's not only a great climber, but also a role model for young girls in Nepal. And she takes risks to help others. A true adventurer.

Gina: Definitely!

Michael: Well, everyone, be sure to vote for this year's Adventurer! That's all for today. Thank you for being with us, Gina. fade out music

Track 2.5 C. **Page 87**

1. An adventurer is often someone who does a dangerous or *extreme* sport like mountain climbing, surfing, or highlining.
2. But someone can be adventurous in their work, too. For example, photographers take pictures of interesting people and places, and explorers travel all over the world and discover many things.
3. Sure! The Adventurer of the Year in 2016, for example, was Pasang Lhamu Sherpa Akita. She's a mountain climber from Nepal. She was one of the first Nepali women to climb K2…

Track 2.6 A. **Page 88**

1. **Michael:** So, first, can you tell everyone what the *Adventurer of the Year* award is?

   Gina: Of course! Each year, National Geographic chooses ten of the best…
2. **Gina:** But they also need to find answers to problems and think quickly, so a good mind is important, too.

   Michael: Absolutely! Great points. So, who votes?
3. **Michael:** I see. Can you give us an example? Tell us about one of the winners.

   Gina: Sure! The Adventurer of the Year in 2016, for example, was Pasang…
4. **Michael:** And she takes risks to help others. A true adventurer.

   Gina: Definitely!

LESSON B Vocabulary

Track 2.7 A. Page 94

count
danger
decrease
discover
forest
goals
protect
wild

Track 2.8 B. Meaning from Context Page 94

Exploration: Risk and Reward

Hundreds of years ago, people built boats and crossed the oceans. In the 1960s, astronauts started traveling to space. And today people continue to go to new places and do things no one has done before. These people risk their lives. Why? What are their goals? Here are a few:

- To learn: An explorer might face danger deep under the ocean, in a thick tropical rain forest, high on a mountain, or even in space in order to learn. Humans naturally want to learn.
- To teach: When explorers discover something and learn about it, they teach us interesting new things. We learn not only about the world, but also about ourselves.
- To protect: When a photographer takes a photo of a crocodile or some other wild animal, the animal becomes more real to us. We want to keep it safe. We count how many there are because we don't want the population to decrease.

Everyone has goals. For many people, learning a job, teaching their children, and protecting their families and homes is enough. But for explorers, it's about changing the world.

Listening: A Conversation about Emma Stokes

Track 2.9 B. Listening for Main Ideas, C. Listening for Details, and D. Page 97

Marcus: Hi, Rebecca. What are you doing?

Rebecca: Reading this story about Emma Stokes, an explorer for National Geographic.

Marcus: What does she do?

Rebecca: She helps protect animals like gorillas in Africa and tigers in Asia. They are in danger and may not be around for much longer.

Marcus: That sounds like an interesting job.

Rebecca: Interesting for sure, but it can be pretty risky, too.

Marcus: What do you mean?

Rebecca: Well, she often hikes through places with these wild animals. She was almost stepped on by elephants once, for example.

Marcus: Whoa! What happened?

Rebecca: She was in the jungle and her team stopped to camp for the night. In the middle of the night, she woke up because she heard screaming and felt heavy footsteps. The ground was moving under her.

Marcus: Yikes!

Rebecca: Yeah, they didn't know it, but they were right in the middle of an elephant path.

Marcus: That's scary! Was she OK?

Rebecca: Yes, luckily, everyone got out of the way in time.

Marcus: Why did she go there?

Rebecca: She went to count the number of gorillas. Her goal was to protect them.

Marcus: Did she find any?

Rebecca: Yes, she actually discovered 125,000. No one knew they were there.

Marcus: Are you serious!? That's a huge number. How did no one know?

Rebecca: Well, Emma and her team were the first scientists to go there. It was difficult to find a way through the forest. They cut a path just wide enough to get through.

Marcus: Where did they sleep?

Rebecca: They often had to sleep in trees.

Marcus: Wow, that does *not* sound like fun, but it's great they found 125,000 gorillas!

Rebecca: Yes, it was wonderful news, but she says that number can decrease very quickly. Emma uses the information she collects to teach companies and local people how to protect the land for the gorillas. If a company wants to cut the trees to sell the wood, or if the gorillas become sick, their numbers could decrease.

Marcus: That's terrible. I'd like to read that story. Where… fade

Track 2.10 A. Page 98

Rebecca: …. In the middle of the night, she woke up because she heard screaming and felt heavy footsteps. The ground was moving under her.

Marcus: Yikes!

Rebecca: Yeah, they didn't know it, but they were right in the middle of an elephant path.

Marcus: That's scary! Was she OK?

Rebecca: Yes, luckily everyone got out of the way in time.

Marcus: Why did she go there?

Rebecca: She went to count the number of gorillas. Her goal was to protect them.

Marcus: Did she find any?

Rebecca: Yes, she actually discovered 125,000. No one knew they were there.

Speaking

Track 2.11 Pronunciation: Simple Past *-ed* Endings Page 99

The *-d/-ed* ending sounds like:

- /əd/ (or /əd/) after verbs ending with /t, d/. This forms a new syllable.
  needed, counted, waited
- /t/ after voiceless consonants (/f, k, p, s, ʃ, tʃ/)
  surfed, hiked, hopped, kissed, washed, watched
- /d/ after voiced consonants /b, g, ð, ʒ, dʒ, l, m, n, ŋ, r, v, z/ and all vowels
  bathed, judged, offered, solved, played

Track 2.12 B. Page 99

/əd/ or /Id/: guided, protected, voted
/t/: camped, helped, jumped, risked
/d/: died, discovered, received

Unit 6: Taking Action

LESSON A Vocabulary

Track 2.13 A. Page 104

according to
believe
especially
habits
reduce
research
throw away
worst

Track 2.14 B. Meaning from Context Page 104

Easy Ways You Can Use Less Plastic

According to many scientists, plastic trash is a big problem. Many say it is the worst problem in our world today. Follow these five easy tips to change your everyday habits with trash.

Tip 1: Stop buying water in plastic bottles. Many people believe bottled water is better than water from your kitchen sink, but research shows that bottled water is often not safer.

Tip 2: Don't use and then throw away plastic utensils. Take a fork, knife, spoon, and/or chopsticks with you.

Tip 3: Take a bag with you to the store. Say 'no' to paper and plastic bags, especially plastic ones.

Tip 4: Buy your food in glass jars. Save the jars and reuse them.

Tip 5: Reduce the number of things you buy and throw away soon after.

Listening: Student Podcast: Oceans of Plastic

Track 2.15 C. Listening for Main Ideas and D. Listening for Details Page 97

Martin: Hello, again. Welcome to my weekly show. I'm Martin Nota. If you listened last week, you learned about the islands of trash in our oceans. The *Great Pacific Garbage Patch,* the biggest of these islands, is in the Pacific Ocean. It's between Japan, Hawaii, and California. It's larger than France. It's unbelievable. And for some reason, we continue to add more trash to it every day!

Today I'm going to talk about the worst type of trash in the ocean: *plastic.* Plastic is especially bad because it takes so long to disappear. This is the stuff almost everything is made of nowadays: drink bottles, cups, plates, forks and spoons, toys, and lots of other things, from phones to furniture. Why do we create so much with plastic? Is it a good thing? Well, let me give you my thoughts on that.

First, for the *Did You Know?* part of the show, here are some facts about plastic.

Did you know:

- that we made more plastic in the last ten years than in *all* of the 1900s?
- that 50% of all the plastic we use is for one-time use? In other words, we throw away half of the plastic we use after only using it once.
- that the average American throws away 185 pounds of plastic a year?
- that Americans throw away 35 billion plastic water bottles every year?
- that people worldwide use more than 1 million plastic bags *each minute*?

Sounds crazy, right? Well, it is! And what does it *mean*? According to one study in Australia, over 90% of the world's sea birds have eaten plastic. Research shows that a million sea birds and around 100,000 other sea animals die *each* year because of plastic trash. Many of these animals believe the plastic is food, so they eat it. Humans, of course, eat a lot of seafood, so *we* are eating the plastic, too!

We are hurting and killing animals. We are hurting and possibly even killing ourselves!

So, what are we going to *do* about it? Many people are trying to find a way to clean the ocean, and that's great, but it's not easy. The problem is getting worse every year. We can't *undo* the past, but we *can* change our habits for the future. The time to reduce the plastic we use is *NOW*.

So, what are *you* going to do about it?

Now, here are some easy tips to follow. Until next week, stay *clean* and go *green!*

Track 2.16 E. Note Taking Page 107

Did you know...

that we made more plastic in the last ten years than in all of the 1900s?

that 50% of all the plastic we use is for one-time use? In other words, we throw away half of the plastic we use after only using it once.

that the average American throws away 185 pounds of plastic a year?

that Americans throw away 35 billion plastic water bottles every year?

that people worldwide use more than 1 million plastic bags each minute?

Track 2.17 F. Page 107

1. The problem is getting worse every year. (passionate)
2. The sea turtle at the animal hospital died. (sad)
3. The time to reduce plastic is NOW. (passionate)
4. We must change our habits. (passionate)
5. I just watched a video about sea birds. (sad)

Speaking

Track 2.18 Pronunciation: *Be Going To (Gonna)* Page 108

A: Hey. Are you gonna speak at the town meeting?

B: No, but I'm gonna be there.

Track 2.19 C. and D. Critical Thinking: Categorizing Page 109

Emily: Hi everyone. Welcome to the second meeting of *Project Clean and Green.* I'm Emily. First, I'm going to read the plans we discussed at last month's meeting. After, we can talk about any new ideas. OK, so:

- First, to clean the air, we're *not* going to plant 100 trees this year; we're going to plant *200!* We're also going to present some clean air ideas from other cities at our monthly meetings. Tonight, Tim's going to talk about a project in Nanjing, China—it's really interesting. By 2018, they're going to have over 3,500 trees and plants growing in, around, and on some very tall buildings.
In fact, we're planning to present a new project at each of our

monthly meetings. Vladimir is going to discuss a project in Ljubljana, Slovenia, next month.

- Next, to reduce trash, Kumiko is going to visit coffee shops and restaurants and pick up any old coffee, fruits, and vegetables. She's also going to teach a class about growing your own food. Let her know if you are interested.
- Finally, to help clean trash near the river, we're going to have *Clean the River* events the first Saturday of every month. I'm going to organize it, so let me know if you want to help.

LESSON B Vocabulary

Track 2.20 A. Page 114

behavior
criminals
garden
guest
increase
pretty
prisons
purpose

Track 2.21 B. Meaning from Context Page 114

Nature Behind Bars

Several universities around the country have projects in nearby prisons. The aim is to help the prisoners learn about nature. The projects send guest speakers, offer classes, or do some type of research. For example, some have started a garden where prisoners can grow food and take notes on different plants and give their notes to scientists. Other projects involve animals. Research shows that working with nature can increase a person's level of happiness.

Further, the work gives prisoners a purpose. They do not usually have much to do in prison and life can be pretty boring. Working on the projects teaches them about gardening and animal behavior.

Very dangerous criminals cannot usually do these activities. However, nature can still help. To test her ideas, one researcher put photos of nature (such as trees and plants) in their prison cells. She wanted to see if it made them happier. The results show that even photos of nature can help people.

Listening: A Conversation about Nalini Nadkarni

Track 2.22 B. Listening for Main Ideas and C. Listening for Details Page 116

Claudi: Hey Jamal. What's up? Do you have any plans for the weekend?

Jamal: Not really. I'm going to study for our science test next week, and maybe play some basketball. How about you?

Claudi: I'm going to see that guest lecturer tonight. My professor told us about it. It sounds so interesting.

Jamal: Wait, I don't think I heard about it. Who's speaking?

Claudi: A biologist; her name is Nalini Nadkarni. She studies trees and other plants that depend on trees. She also does a lot to increase people's interest in nature.

Jamal: Oh, wait—is she the one who did that project with city kids and a rap musician? She took them into the forest. Then the kids worked with a rap musician to create music about it?

Claudi: Yes! That's her. She's going to talk about another project she helped start in prisons.

Jamal: Yeah, I heard about that. I read that she even worked with very dangerous criminals. She looked at the effect of photos on their behavior or something? I think she discovered that just *seeing* photos of trees reduced the number of fights.

Claudi: Yep. That's right. It's pretty amazing. Other prisoners helped with plants and animals. They took daily notes for her research. She saw that these activities helped the prisoners. They enjoyed having a purpose. Now, many prisoners help keep a garden or do other work with nature. I guess it can be pretty boring to be in prison with nothing to do. Anyway, it helped them, but it also helped her learn about the plants and animals. It seems like a win-win project.

Jamal: Absolutely! That's such a great idea.

Claudi: Hey, I've got to run. I've got class in a few minutes, but you should come tonight! It starts at six thirty, but I'm going to get there around five thirty so I can get a good seat.

Jamal: Yeah, I think I will. Sounds fun. I'll see you there!

Unit 7: Lost and Found

LESSON A Vocabulary

Track 2.23 A. Page 124

find
gold
hide
jewels
missing
mystery
objects noun
search

Track 2.24 B. Meaning from Context Page 124

Lost Treasure: Fabergé Eggs

In cultures around the world, an egg is a symbol that means new life, birth, or springtime. For thousands of years, people all over the world have colored or decorated eggs.

In 1885, Alexander III, the Tsar (or King) of Russia, wanted to give his wife a special gift, so he asked the famous artist Peter Carl Fabergé to make an egg with gold and jewels. His wife loved the egg so much that he gave her a new one every year. They had 50 of these beautiful objects when the Tsar and his family were killed during the Russian Revolution· but at some point, they disappeared. Did someone take the eggs? Did the Tsar hide them? Today, 43 of the eggs were found and are in museums around the world, but there are still seven missing eggs. Each egg is probably worth millions of dollars today! Nobody knows where these eggs are, but many search for them. It's a complete mystery. Who will be the first person to find one?

Listening: Interview with a Treasure Hunter

Track 2.25 B. Listening for Main Ideas and C. Listening for Details Page 126–127

Podcast host: People love mystery, discovery, and exploration. As children, we play hide and seek; we hide things from others and we love to look for treasure, but for some, this love continues into adulthood. Today we're talking with a treasure hunter to find out why. So, tell us, why?

Guest: Because it's fun! It's exciting to search for something and then find it!

Podcast host: Yes, treasure hunting is a popular hobby. Nowadays, there are even game apps for your phone. My 13-year-old loves *Pokémon Go*!

Guest: I like that game, too, but I prefer *real* treasure hunts.

Podcast host: Yes. Tell us about that. How did you start?

Guest: It started when I was a child. My mom's ring was missing. She searched everywhere for it. So, I thought I could help her. I asked her some questions—you know, like 'where did she see the ring last;' 'where did she wear the ring last'—those kinds of questions. Then, I took all of this information and found the missing ring! My mom was so happy. It was my first treasure and it was just the beginning.

Podcast host: What other treasures have you found?

Guest: Well, treasure hunting is definitely my hobby, but I didn't say that I was very good at it! Over the years, I have found a few things, like gold and some precious stones. But, I'm searching for one of the biggest treasures in history.

Podcast host: Ah, yes. Forrest Fenn's treasure. Tell us about that.

Guest: Well, Forrest Fenn is a rich man who hid a treasure for people to find.

Podcast host: What's in the treasure?

Guest: A lot of things, but to name a few: gold, some very old coins, jewels, and gemstones. The treasure weighs 42 pounds and is worth around a million dollars.

Podcast host: How do people hunt for it? Is there a map or something?

Guest: Yes. He wrote a book called *The Thrill of the Chase* and it has a map and some information about how to find the treasure.

Podcast host: Why did he do this?

Guest: He did it because he was sick and thought he was dying. He also did it because he wanted to give people the joy of adventure. Nobody has found it yet, but many people are searching for it.

Podcast host: That's amazing!

Guest: He also said he hid the treasure because he wants people to get out of their houses, go outside, and be in nature. You see, to Forrest Fenn, the hunt *is* the treasure.

Podcast host: What do you mean?

Guest: Looking for the treasure is the best part. Even better than finding the objects you are searching for.

Podcast host: Do you agree with him?

Guest: Definitely! Of course, finding a treasure can be exciting, but I don't do this to get rich. I do it because the hunt is exciting.

Podcast host: I agree. Well, thank you for joining us today. After listening to this story, I want to get outside and search for some lost treasure! Fade...

Speaking

Track 2.26 Pronunciation: *Wh*-Question Intonation — Page 128

Where did he hide it?

How did she find the missing objects?

When did they lose the jewels?

LESSON B Vocabulary

Track 2.27 A. — Page 134

ancient

century

culture

history

information

peace

religion

rules

Track 2.28 B. Meaning from Context — Page 134

A Trip to the British Museum

A: How was the British Museum?

B: It was amazing. You know that I love history and learning about the past.

A: Where did you go in the museum?

B: Well, I started in the Asia Gallery. I really like Japanese culture and learning about their way of life.

A: What did you see there?

B: I saw ancient Samurai armor from the 16th century.

A: Oh, that's interesting! I want to see that. Did you take a picture? Or is that against the rules?

B: No, it's allowed! Here's a Greek sculpture from the Parthenon in Athens!

A: That's a great picture! You know, I am interested in early religion. Do they have any Buddhist objects?

B: Yes, they do. You can get a map and more information at the desk just inside the entrance.

A: Great. Thanks! I think I'll go next week. I need to take a break from school.

B: Good idea. You can always find peace and quiet at the museum. It's very relaxing.

Listening: A Guided Tour of the British Museum

Track 2.29 B. Listening for Main Ideas, C. Listening for Details, and D. Note Taking — Pages 136–137

Guide: Please gather around. The tour is about to begin. First of all, I would like to welcome you to the British Museum. We are one of the largest museums in the world, with over 8 million objects from human culture from the past to the present. Please remember to follow all the museum rules: no food or drink and so on. Are there any questions before we get started on our tour?

Tourist #1: Yes. When you say objects from human culture, what do you mean?

Guide: What I mean is these are objects that people have used throughout history, —from the clothes ancient Egyptians such as King Tut wore, to a Samurai helmet used in Japan in the 16th century. These are all objects that humans have used at some time in history. Any other questions? OK, then let's begin our tour.

We'll start in this room, which has objects from ancient Persia. Cyrus the Great started the first Persian Empire in the 6th century BC. It was a large and powerful kingdom. Before he was king, there were many wars and many people died.

In the center of the room is the Cyrus Cylinder. King Cyrus created this in 539 BC. It is a clay tablet with writing on it. On the cylinder,

King Cyrus wrote information about the life and the laws in his kingdom. Many people say that Cyrus was the first leader to write about human rights. Are there any questions so far?

Tourist #2: Yes, I have one. What kind of human rights did he write about?

Guide: Good question. On the cylinder, Cyrus tells the people not to be afraid because in his new kingdom they can live together in peace. He wrote that people from different cultures and religions were welcome and all should live in peace together. He was a very wise man and his cylinder, the Cyrus Cylinder, is an amazing treasure. Are there any more questions?

Tourist #3: Yes, when was the Cyrus Cylinder found?

Guide: An archaeologist, Hormuzd Rassam, found the cylinder in 1879 in Mesopotamia—The British Museum acquired it in 1880. This ancient treasure, from thousands of years ago, is something that we can learn from even today. If you would like more information on the Cyrus Cylinder, the gift shop has an excellent book about it. Moving on to this next room, ...

Unit 8: Breakthroughs

LESSON A Vocabulary

Track 2.30 A. Page 144

become
control
copy
exist
expensive
latest
machine
several

Track 2.31 B. Meaning from Context Page 144

1. There are several ways DNA is used nowadays.
2. Each student has a copy of the same test. There are no differences.
3. A robot is a type of machine; it is not a living thing.
4. I can control the robot by talking to it.
5. The toy robot dog is over $100; it's expensive.
6. He preferred teaching, so he didn't become an engineer.
7. Everyone wants the latest smartphone because they think it's better than the last.
8. Smartphones didn't exist before 2000.

Listening: A Class Discussion about Cloning

Track 2.32 B. Listening for Main Ideas and C. Listening for Details Page 128

Professor: Good afternoon, everyone. How are you today? ….. So, I was wondering, have any of you seen the *Jurassic Park* movies? The latest one, *Jurassic World,* came out just a few years ago.

Student 1: Yes, I saw it. That's the one with the dinosaurs, right?

Professor: Yep, that's right. Do you remember the story? Where did the dinosaurs come from?

Student 1: Um, I think a scientist created the dinosaurs.

Professor: Yes, that's right. He made the dinosaurs in a lab, or he *cloned* them. Basically, *cloning* means that you make a copy of something.

Student 2: So they weren't machines or robots?

Professor: No, they weren't. They were *real.* He used actual *DNA* from the blood of a real dinosaur. So, I bet you can guess the topic for today? I'd like to discuss cloning, but in *real life.*

Student 1: But that was a movie. Scientists can't clone dinosaurs, or any extinct animal, can they?

Professor: No they can't, but …

Student 2: Excuse me professor, but what does *extinct* mean?

Professor: *Extinct* describes animals or plants that don't exist anymore. We also say they *died out.* Dinosaurs are extinct, for example. The last dinosaur lived 65 million years ago. And as you've learned, many plants and animals today are in danger. Some of them will probably become extinct in the future. So, can scientists clone animals?

Student 1: There was a sheep back in the 90s?

Professor: Yes, that's right. In 1996, Dolly was born in Scotland. That was the first time scientists cloned a mammal. She lived around six years. Since then, they have cloned several more sheep.

Student 2: But sheep are around today. Can scientists clone animals that *aren't* around anymore?

Professor: Well, yes and no. Scientists say they can bring back *some* extinct animals but *not* animals as old as dinosaurs. First, though, let me ask you another question. Do you think it is a good *idea* to clone extinct animals?

Student 2: No! I don't think it's a good idea at all. The animals are extinct for a reason. If they come back, they might hurt people.

Student 1: But what about animals like gorillas or elephants? They are in danger, and we don't want to lose them. I think it's a good idea to clone them so they don't *become* extinct.

Student 3: I'm not sure it's a good idea to clone extinct animals. Often, there are problems when people try to control nature. Plus, I bet it's really expensive. Scientists could use the money to help cure illness or something. I don't think we should bring animals back.

Professor: Okay, okay. So cloning might have some good and bad points. For homework…fade

Track 2.33 D. and E. Note Taking Page 147

1

Professor: Well, yes and no. Scientists say they can bring back *some* extinct animals but not animals as old as dinosaurs. First, though, let me ask you another question. Do you think it is a good *idea* to clone extinct animals?

Student 2: No! I don't think it's a good idea at all. The animals are extinct for a reason. If they come back, they might hurt people.

2

Student 1: But what about animals like gorillas or elephants? They are in danger, and we don't want to lose them. I think it's a good idea to clone them so they don't *become* extinct.

3

Student 3: I'm not sure it's a good idea to clone extinct animals. Often, there are problems when people try to control nature. Plus, I bet it's really expensive.

4

Student 3: Scientists could use the money to help cure illness or something. I don't think we should bring animals back.

fade

Speaking

Track 2.34 A. Page 148

Cloning Your Cat: A Good Idea?

In 2001, scientists at Texas A&M University cloned the first pet: C.C. the cat. Since then, cloning has become easier. This could mean big changes in the future.

Many pet lovers might start cloning their cats or dogs. Pet cloning companies could make a lot of money. There was one problem with C.C. the cat, though: she and her clone did not look the same. DNA does not always control a cat's color. C.C. had the same DNA, but the two cats were different colors. People may not want to risk getting a different-looking pet. Also, pet cloning costs from $50,000-$100,000 Most people won't want to spend so much money. And, after all, they could just go to a shelter and get a pet for free.

Finally, many other people won't like the idea of cloning because animals may get hurt. What do *you* think?

Track 2.35 D. and E. Page 150

Lara: Class was interesting today, wasn't it? I didn't know about cloning extinct animals. To be honest, I'm not sure it's a good idea.

Andy: I agree. But I think it's interesting.

Lara: I think it's scary!

Andy: Maybe, but I think cloning a pet might be OK. I read about it the other day. There are several companies that will do it for you.

Lara: Really? Wow! I *do* love my cat. How does that work?

Andy: Well, they put your cat's DNA into an empty egg. Then they put the egg into a female cat, and she gives birth to your cat's clone.

Lara: Wow! That's amazing! And my new cat is *exactly* the same?

Andy: Well, actually, cloned cats may not look the same. The color of a cat does not depend only on its DNA. There are other reasons a cat might be brown or gray, or whatever.

Lara: Really? That's strange. Is their behavior the same?

Andy: Well, in some ways, yes. But in others, it may not be. Their mothers and their life experiences are different, so their behavior could be different, too.

Lara: Hmm.

Andy: Oh, also, it costs around 50 to 100 thousand dollars! It's a bit expensive!

Lara: Woah! And there are so many cats that need homes. I think it's better to get one that is already alive and needs a home.

Andy: Good point.

LESSON B Vocabulary

Track 2.36 A. Page 154

bone
consider
healthy
heart
parts
replace
simple
treatment

Track 2.37 B. Meaning from Context Pages 154–155

Science News Now

3-D Body Parts!

Scientists say they can now print live body parts on 3-D printers. If you need a new arm or leg bone, for example, doctors might soon be able to replace yours with one from a 3-D printer. They may also be able to print an organ such as a stomach or a heart. For more information, ...

New Treatment to Help You See!

Do you know someone who is blind or has poor vision? A new treatment is now available. It is helping many people to see again. Consider the changes it could bring to their lives. For more information, ...

Cheap DNA Tests!

Are you going to be healthy in the future? Find out with cheap DNA tests. Learn about your DNA for *just* $100! Several companies will do a simple test for you. Soon after, they will send you the results. With this information, you can learn about your genes. You can see if you are healthy. You can also research your family and find cousins you didn't know about. For more information, ...

Listening: A Lecture on Ending Blindness

Track 2.38 B. Listening for Main Ideas (Part I) Page 156

Hello. Welcome to State University's Massive Open Online Course from the Health and Science Department. Today's lecture is about blindness, or rather, a future *without* blindness.

How can we help people who cannot see? Well, the treatment that 50 percent of these people need is simple. In other words, *half* of all blind people could see *today*, but many are not able to go to a doctor. For the other half, this is not an easy question to answer. There are many reasons for blindness. But with more time and research, scientists now believe we can end it within the next 20 years.

They believe that these three treatments, once they are perfect, will bring an end to all kinds of blindness: cell therapy, stem cells, and bionic eye parts. Before I discuss the three treatments, let's consider the problem.

Do you know how many people in the world are blind, or cannot see at all? 39 million people world-wide. That's about one in every 200 people. Another 246 million people have great difficulty seeing. Where are these people? Well, 90 percent live in low-income countries. This is a problem of the poor.

Track 2.39 C. Listening for Main Ideas (Part 2) Page 157

So, first I will briefly describe the three exciting treatments that many believe will end all blindness. Then, we will look at each treatment in more detail.

First, Cell Therapy: Remember we discussed cells before. A cell is the smallest part of a living thing (a human, animal, or plant). Each cell has DNA. Your genes are part of your DNA and they carry information about your body. You get your genes from your parents, grandparents, and all before them. Your genes make you *you.* Sometimes, your cells might not work properly, so with cell therapy, a doctor replaces the unhealthy eye cells with healthy ones.

Second, Stem Cells: We just discussed replacing eye cells. Well, each part of the body has its own cells. Eye cells, and, for example, blood cells, heart cells, skin cells, bone cells, and so on. A *stem* cell is a simple cell before it becomes an eye cell or any of these other types. Everyone has stem cells in addition to these other cells.

Some blind people are born without a part of their eye; others have some other problem. With stem cell treatment, a doctor puts stem cells in the eye, and the stem cells grow and *become* the missing cells.

Third, Bionic Eye Parts: As you probably know, people who lose an arm or a leg can, nowadays, get a *bionic* arm or leg. This is an arm or leg machine. People learn to control the bionic arm or leg with their brain. A similar idea, but much smaller, is to replace an unhealthy part of an eye with a small machine, or bionic eye part.

These ideas do not yet work all the time, but as I mentioned, they may help end blindness in the next twenty years. That's all for today. Next time, we'll look at Cell Therapy in more detail.

Track 2.40 D. Listening for Details (Whole lecture) Page 157

See previous two tracks (2.38 and 2.39 together).

Speaking

Track 2.41 Pronunciation: Schwa in Unstressed Syllables Page 158

be**come** ma**chine** re**place**

*The patient can kən **see** now.*

*The company could cəd **earn** over one million dollars this year.*

Track 2.42 A. Page 158

1. bi**o**logy
2. tech**no**logy
3. **ther**apy
4. **pro**blem
5. com**pu**ter
6. **sci**entist
7. con**trol**
8. **cri**minal

Track 2.43 B. Page 158

New Breakthrough in Fighting Crime

Scientists are using DNA from crime scenes in a new way. They are becoming better at understanding the meaning of genes every year. By looking at the DNA, they can tell us hair color, face shape, and other information about a person's body. In many police stations around the United States, computer programmers can create a face that may look like the person who did the crime. This is amazing technology, but could it be dangerous? What do *you* think?

VIDEO SCRIPTS

UNIT 1 Coming of Age

Narrator: Around the world, every child becomes an adult in a different way. Yoro Sisse is a 16-year-old Fulani boy from Diafarabe, Mali. Every year, teams of young Fulani boys, like Yoro, make a long trip. They do this to find food for their cows. During the dry season, the cows can stay near the Fulani's home. But in the wet season, there is too much rain for the cows to stay there. They take their cows into the Sahel, near the Sahara Desert. In the desert, there aren't many trees or plants. It is very dry. The boys travel along the edge of the desert, moving from place to place.

The boys' trip can take almost eight months. There is little food for the boys near the desert. They do not carry a lot of food with them. They usually only drink milk.

Yoro: We have to keep moving to find more food for our cows. Our job is to bring back fat cows.

Narrator: This is something every Fulani boy has to do. It's a very important job. When Yoro goes home, everyone will look at his cows. If the cows are all OK, the other Fulani people will know Yoro can take good care of his herd. Then, they will say he is not a boy, but a man. This is Yoro's girlfriend, Aissa. She wants him to come back with good cows because she wants to marry him. In the Fulani tribe, mothers and fathers choose the person their children can marry. If Yoro doesn't come back with good cows, Aissa's parents won't let her marry him.

During the trip, Yoro thinks about many things. He worries about finding food for his cows. He also worries about other people who want to take the cows. Yoro starts his journey in Diafarabe, Mali. He takes his cows through Mauritania, to the Sahel. The Fulani people have walked this way for thousands of years. Yoro has walked for three months. Now he is going back to his home, and his family, and his girlfriend.

Yoro: We walk all day without stopping. Sometimes we get very thirsty and the cows get tired. Often, we don't sleep at night.

Narrator: The young cows in Yoro's herd look good. Everyone can see Yoro's hard work. He marks them so everyone knows they are his. The trip is almost over, and Yoro is excited to see his girlfriend. But now, they still have to cross the river. Yoro swims with his cows. He wants to make sure they are OK. Across the river, his family and friends wait for the boys. After a long and difficult trip, Yoro's cows are all OK. It's time to celebrate and have fun.

UNIT 2 Wanted: Adventure Storyteller

Fitz Cahall: There wasn't really a job description for what I wanted to do. You know, people don't hire storytellers, much less adventure storytellers. That was my dream.

I mean, I was that six-year-old kid you'd see with his face buried in National Geographics. I knew there was magic in life on the road. I love climbing. I love being outside. I would load all this stuff up into my car, leave the city, and I'd spend a couple months out on the road. And then I'd come back home, and I'd write it all down.

But I wound up with all these stories I'd gathered from my time on the road. And I just – I couldn't sell them anywhere.

I was about to give up when I had this realization that nobody was going to give me this job. I had to go create it.

Once I realized that, it was like the horizon opened up. I started a radio show in my closet. I went on to make films. We found our community.

It's seven years later, and I'm still basically doing the same thing. I go hit the road, and I go spend time with the people that inspire me, in places that inspire me. That process has come full circle right back to where my dream started.

When National Geographic asked me to help with Adventurers of the Year, the six-year-old boy in me kind of chuckled. We pulled together ten incredible stories, ten incredible feats from people who live life on their own terms. I think it would be easy to put these people up on a pedestal and to think of them as heroes or almost superhuman. And while talent plays a role in these people's feats and their successes, it's not what makes their ideas a reality. It's grit, creativity, passion, kindness, and love. That's the human spirit.

I know in my heart I could be an Adventurer of the Year, but that's not what I want to do. I want to tell stories, spend as much as time as I can outside, and pass that love for it along to my son.

My struggles to make my dreams a reality have taken just as much commitment as paddling into a big wave or climbing a peak in the Karakoram. There's a lot of ways to take risks in life. That's the magic of it.

I know this. You have to do the thing that makes you tick. You have to do it on a daily basis. You have to do it unapologetically. Do it with love.

UNIT 3 Monkey City

Narrator: Lopburi, Thailand, is famous for its monkeys. Every year on the last Sunday in November, the Lopburi Inn, a local hotel, sponsors a festival just for the resident macaque monkeys. And there are lots of them. For the Thai people, monkeys are very important. They believe that a monkey called Hanuman helped them in the past.

Nathanicha Kitwatananusont: We believe that Hanuman never dies. So, he is a symbol of prosperity and good luck.

Narrator: The monkeys even walk around right next to the people. Every day, the people from the town bring the monkeys food. But on the day of the festival, they bring a lot of food. The people watch while the monkeys eat all the food. Even the statues of monkeys get food and a bottle of water.

The sponsor of all this monkey business, Mr. Yongyuth, knows how to make an entrance. The first goal of the festival is to bring food to the monkeys.

Professor Phibul: But the second is for the tourists. Every year, a lot of people, many people come to the Lopburi to see the monkey party.

Narrator: The monkeys are very naughty. They eat and play all day and they never take a nap.

Nathanicha Kitwatananusont: You never get them to sit still. That's for sure.

Matt Sayles (Tourist): I was kneeling down taking picture of a monkey and all of a sudden a monkey swiped my – my sunglasses off.

Narrator: The monkeys are a problem for the tourists and they are also a problem for the people of Lopburi.

Man: I just frighten the monkeys. I don't kill them.

Narrator: Thai people like monkeys. They are not dangerous. But they sometimes cut the electrical and telephone cables. That is the problem. But the people of Lopburi are happy to live with the monkeys. They like the monkeys and they give them food every day. The monkeys even take food from people's hands. People also wear costumes and decorate the city.

Nathanicha Kitwatananusont: When people come to visit here, you could see the smile on their face.

Professor Phibul: Next year it'll be bigger than this year. Sure.

Narrator: The people love the monkey party.

UNIT 4 High Tech or No Tech?

Man 1: ... how much more I spend on my phone than what I used to is ridiculous.

Man 2: I look at my – like little brothers and stuff.

Woman 1: There are definitely weekends where me and him will sit inside and play on our computers.

Man 2: All they do is sit on like video games and the computer. I technically do too for a living.

Woman 2: Technology isn't the enemy. I think it can help bring people into parks too, if you let them know.

Woman 3: My generation is a reconnaissance to the wilderness. And I think that is spurred by social media.

Man 3: Is the point for me to share this with people on the Internet of what – look what I did and isn't this great?

Woman 4: The people in my generation who come through – kind of have a checklist, is what I've noticed.

Woman 3: Oh, this spot. This spot. This spot, I'm going to go there.

Man 3: Or is it to inspire other people to get out?

Woman 5: The different way that we're experiencing parks is that we're doing it in a more interactive way. So we'll Tweet it, we'll Instagram it.

Woman 1: We use Google Maps to find all sorts of parks to go camping in.

Man 4: ... Airbnb

Man 5: And you can go look at trails on topo maps.

Man 6: You know, I use birding apps to identify birds.

Man 7: It's easier than ever.

Woman 6: The question is, where's the line?

Man 8: There's always this debate of people who are like ...

Woman 6: How much are you actually looking at what you're seeing?

Woman 7: Even though they're in nature, they're seeing it still through a screen.

Man 8: When I've tried that before, I've not taken my camera out, and I'll see a beautiful sunset or something and then I just regret it.

Man 9: For me personally, it's a motivator.

Man 8: I can really appreciate what I'm seeing while capturing it. And I like to have those memories and I love that social media can have – can capture those moments.

Man 9: I see something cool and I want to take a picture of it or I want to film it or something like that then I'm going to go out further.

Man 6: Meanwhile, people are crashing drones into thermal features in Yellowstone so, yeah.

Woman 5: If you have WiFi at a park, sometimes you'll see the kids sitting around the visitor center.

Woman 8: There's a lot of visitors that come here that are so wrapped up into technology.

Woman 5: Tweeting about it and they don't really want to walk anywhere maybe.

Woman 8: They don't realize when they come to Yosemite National Park that it's basically a black hole for all cell phone service.

Man 5: People are afraid to be alone in nature without anything to occupy their time.

Woman 8: And then that's when they start to realize: wow there's like more to life than technology.

Woman 5: At the same time, someone's going to see their Tweet who's never been to a park.

Woman 9: One person goes and visits it and then they get to see pictures, and they get to see how much you enjoyed it.

Man 10: People are constantly kind of bombarded with images of these places and it makes them want to go.

Woman 3: The more you see it, the more accessible it feels.

Woman 10: We're on Instagram like ...(yeah) Oh, let's go here. Let's go here.

Man 11: I can't even tell you since I've lived here how many people have reached out to me.

Woman 8: On like social media that don't know me at all. Like wow, like you live such an amazing life.

Man 11: Hey, I've never been to Yosemite before but I really want to go.

Man 6: In the future, maybe some of the visitation in national parks will be virtually.

Man 11: It's one thing to have it with technology ...

Man 8: ... and that's probably fine.

Man 11: It's another thing to live it and they say "authentically experience it."

Man 8: The eco-systems don't care. They'll still be here.

UNIT 5 Highlining Yosemite Falls

Dean Potter, Yosemite Valley

Late Spring, 2011

Dean Potter: My name's Dean Potter and I live right here in Yosemite Valley. I've been living here 17 years. This line is one of the hardest lines that I've tried to walk. The moving water, the wind—there's a lot of distractions.

Yosemite, it really brings out my creativity. It's such a powerful place, there's some sort of amazing energy going on that fuels me. Late spring, early summer—it's the perfect time for releasing this massive gush of water over the falls.

I have to be totally analytical to rig a line that's not going to fail. There's a lot of air right here. I don't want to be thinking about line failure or anything. That's why I have this incredible gear, hundred-thousand-pound shackle, makes me feel warm and fuzzy. This stuff called Amsteel, so it's this soft cable. It's 40 percent stronger than steel, but it floats. A whole new level, man. It's kinda new for slacklining for people to pull lines with the grip hoist, but it's something that tightrope walkers have done probably close to a century.

People just think I'm a lunatic or an adrenaline junkie, and that's not really what's going on with me. The beauty is mostly what I'm concerned with, and that's really why I'm up here trying to cross a line over Yosemite Falls.

I'll just focus on the beauty and on my breath but that water doesn't stop. Like, I wish I had blinders on. Something moving so drastically in my field of vision—it's a huge challenge for me.

I'm getting blinded by spray. I'll try one more time, really focus.

I was just getting rocked around by the wind and blinded by the spray of the waterfall. Yeah, I was supposed to fall, but somehow I stood back up and kept going.

When I'm out on the line, it really brings out my creativity. And for me, pushing into the unknown is a big part of what I call fun. Seeing a new part of yourself that you didn't know was there.

This is when it's fun: right now.

You know if you're lucky… brief moments when you're just seeing everything, seeing the beautiful world, all that's there, right in the moment.

In memory of Dean Potter

April 14, 1972- May, 16, 2015

UNIT 6 Choices

Part 1

Woman: The past year, I have made a journey across this country. I was quite amazed by what I saw. I had never imagined it would be like this. This is the legacy we have created. This is the image of our home we present to the world. I think of future generations and their feelings encountering scenes like this. This is what many places in the country look like. These views, these scenes… These are the memories I will carry with me forever. It has been a profound experience traveling here. It has made me look at my land in new ways. My expectations have met the reality of this country, a reality hard to describe, extraordinary to experience, impossible to forget. I can only wonder, will this ever change?

The choice is ours.

Part 2

Woman: The past year, I have made a journey across this country. I was quite amazed by what I saw. I had never imagined it would be like this. This is the legacy we have created. This is the image of our home we present to the world. I think of future generations and their feelings encountering scenes like this. This is what many places in the country look like. These views, these scenes… These are the memories I will carry with me forever. It has been a profound experience traveling here. It has made me look at my land in new ways. My expectations have met the reality of this country, a reality hard to describe, extraordinary to experience, impossible to forget. I can only wonder, will this ever change?

The choice is ours.

UNIT 7 Dinosaur Detective

Nizar Ibrahim: I'm going to take you on a journey back in time. I'm not talking about 500 years, 2000 years, no. I'm taking you back in deep time, to a lost world of African dinosaurs, a place that is far more bizarre than any other ecosystem we know of.

The Sahara is a magical place – both beautiful and frightening, peaceful and cruel, almost like a world of its own. Today, this is a sea of sand, but a hundred million years ago this place was a huge river system.

When I was about 25 years old, I began a fieldwork project to collect fossils in the border region between Morocco and Algeria. People told me that I'm crazy. But I think, in science, you sometimes have to be crazy. I think you need people to push the boundaries; I mean, that's what science is about.

People thought I would never find anything significant. Well, we found a few things. This is the actual site where a partial skeleton of Spinosaurus was found. Let's see if we can find something new.

I never fully understood the concept of deep time until I found an ancient piece of riverbed in the Sahara, little pebbles, and a dinosaur tooth. And all these objects were arranged in the same direction of flow. This scene just came to life in my mind: a dinosaur upstream, losing a tooth, and the tooth is just rolling on the riverbed, it's carried downstream and it suddenly gets stuck in this little sand dune, in the river. I had, in my hands, a snapshot of time, from a time when humans were absent on our planet.

Excerpt for Exercise C

I never fully understood the concept of deep time until I found an ancient piece of riverbed in the Sahara, little pebbles, and a dinosaur tooth. And all these objects were arranged in the same direction of flow. This scene just came to life in my mind: a dinosaur upstream, losing a tooth, and the tooth is just rolling on the riverbed, it's carried downstream and it suddenly gets stuck in this little sand dune, in the river. I had, in my hands, a snapshot of time, from a time when humans were absent on our planet.

UNIT 8 A Chance to See Again

Radio Announcer: I'm here to tell our people that we are going to have an eye camp at Oshakati State Hospital. So we are telling all of our listeners that we have got one month for you to come to the hospital for your screening. Bring your uncle. Bring your grandmother. Bring everybody to come. This is your chance to see again.

Dr. Helena Ndume: When I started the eye camp, just 82 patients came. Because they say, "If you go there, that young girl is going to destroy your eyes." But then the 82 that we operated on spread the message like wildfire. The following year, we couldn't control the crowd. They came in the thousands.

You cannot just be in a private practice, making money, knowing very well there are thousands who are blind. And they need help. No money in this world can pay for the happiness of someone who was blind. And suddenly, you take off that eye patch and they say, "Doctor, I can see." We have to have a culture of giving back to less fortunate people so that they can be transformed.